A GUIDE TO
WORKING IN EUROPE

A Guide to
WORKING
IN
EUROPE

Jessica Classon

THE MERCIER PRESS
CORK & DUBLIN

The Mercier Press
4 Bridge Street, Cork, &
24 Lower Abbey Street, Dublin 1

British Library Cataloguing in Publication Data
Classon, Jessica
   A Guide to Working in Europe
   1. European community countries. Employment
   I. Title
   331.12'5'094

ISBN 0 85342 893 X

For
Fiachra Ó Marcaigh
with thanks

Typeset by: Seton Music Graphics Ltd., Bantry, Co. Cork.
Printed by The Leinster Leader Ltd., Naas, Co. Kildare.

CONTENTS

ACKNOWLEDGEMENTS

The author wishes to thank the following people and organisations for their assistance in compiling this book: Margaret Caulder, Valerie Cotter, Aideen Damery, L. Declerck, Anne Farrelly, Fergus, Ger Siggins, Olé Guldberg, M. Larrotcha, Rosemary McCarthy, Brendan O'Dea, Siobhan Phillips, Jim Reid, Breda Ryder, Gitta Wemssen, M. Engin Yazicioğlu, The Austrian Embassy, The Belgian Embassy, The Royal Danish Embassy, The French Embassy, The Embassy of the Federal Republic of Germany, The Embassy of Greece, The Italian Embassy, The Royal Netherlands Embassy, The Norwegian Embassy, The Spanish Embassy, The Swedish Embassy, The Embassy of Switzerland, The Consulate General for The Republic of Turkey, Carole Devaney of The Mercier Press and last, but by no means least, Peter Sutherland, former European Commissioner, for writing the Preface to this book.

Preface

The opportunities for young people to work in mainland Europe have never been greater and they are likely to increase rather than diminish in the future. The startling demographic trends and the lack of vitally skilled people provide an opportunity, however, which can only be availed of by those who have acquired the linguistic skills and the familiarity with other cultures which will enable them to adapt to a different environment.

One of the more fundamental difficulties faced by anyone contemplating working on mainland Europe is lack of basic knowledge. This book sets out to remedy that deficiency and does so in a very competent and complete manner. I think that it will be an invaluable reference work for many.

I hope and believe that many of those who have found it necessary to avail of this book and to work abroad will use the skills they learn and will return to enrich the cultural and economic life of this country.

Peter Sutherland
European Commissioner (1985-88)
Dublin, April 1989

Introduction

Fed up? Sick of your job? Or no job at all? Or a job that uses none of your skills? Or competing in a job market where all you seem to get is a nominal interview and no more? Or let's say you are working and are lucky enough to be well-paid — what then? What do you think of your lifestyle? What are your chances of recognition and promotion?

Or do you want to gain valuable work experience in another country? Improve your languages? Want to see how other people do things? Maybe bring your skills back home and set up your own business?

This book is for anyone who is thinking of going to live and work in continental Europe. It is an introduction to what is on offer abroad, the countries you may work in, their visa or residence permit requirements, the work areas with openings and the things to consider when choosing where to go. It also gives information about ways of finding work from your present base in Ireland, the qualifications most in demand and some of the sponsored schemes available.

The book covers 16 European countries, selected on the basis of the work opportunities they currently offer. Ten EC countries are dealt with — Belgium, Denmark, France, Germany, Greece, Italy, Luxembourg, the Netherlands, Portugal and Spain. (The UK is not included here since our nearest neighbour has been a familiar destination for generations. There are no work restrictions between Ireland and Britain, nor are there linguistic and bureaucratic obstacles of the kind that are necessary to deal with when going to mainland Europe.) Six non-EC European countries are also included — Austria, Finland, Norway, Sweden, Switzerland and Turkey. There is background information on each of the countries and a review of the local systems for legal residence, tax, social insurance and health care.

The EC or European Community is considered in detail, with a special look at the organisations and systems which should help us to make the most of our freedom of access to other countries and the real advantages our membership gives. The opportunities

10

for job-seeking and living Community-wide are included, together with the background rules and regulations. Too little is still known about the detailed requirements for foreign workers in other EC countries, despite all the talk about 1992. This book aims to make the picture clearer.

Making the most of your assets: In many cases, especially in the service industries, far more time and effort is required of people abroad than an Irish employer currently demands. The compensation for long days of hard work is often a higher standard of living and greater opportunities for advancement. The bottom line is that most people would rather work hard for reward and recognition than not find a job at all, whether in their own country or elsewhere. There are countries that will give your skills their due.

This book looks at some of them and the red tape you have to go through to live and work elsewhere — legally. It mentions ways and means you can go about getting there from this end — and even how to find someone who will pay you to do so. It examines the preparations you can make to maximise your chances and it casts an eye over the systems of tax and health care you will be going into, as well as giving a little background information on each destination.

THE OFFICIAL STORY

The information in this book on visa regulations, work and residence permits and the requirements of different countries' tax, health and welfare systems is written on the basis of publications and information provided by the embassies of the countries involved. The EC regulations, further information sources and sponsored schemes mentioned are publicised either by official agencies or government departments.

Times change, regulations are altered and responsibility shifts from one agency or department to another. Policies change, too, and it is easy to misinterpret the effects of often complex rules or policies, as they are written, on an individual case.

Every effort has been made to ensure an accurate reflection of current procedure. But, when in doubt, there is nothing better than checking directly. The addresses and telephone numbers of the relevant agencies, embassies and organisations in Ireland and abroad are listed at the back of the book and there are also suggestions for further reading.

As we all know, the difference between what is supposed to happen and what actually happens in practice is often wide. The information in these pages attempts to provide the official position and the official regulations. You may find reality is very different and your own situation more complex or more straightforward. It helps, however, to know the rules when you are actually face-to-face with an official. You can even choose to ignore the more nit-picking or apparently unnecessary regulations.

The choice is yours, but it is hoped that this information will make it easier to close the gap between theory and reality when dealing with officialdom.

1
Starting Out

THE FACTS

The Union Bank of Switzerland conducted a survey in October 1988 of living costs in 52 cities worldwide. The conclusion — only Tokyo, Oslo, Helsinki, Stockholm, Copenhagen, Geneva and Zurich were more expensive than Dublin. A selection of 111 items was costed (including foodstuffs, beverages, tobacco products, personal care articles, clothing, household appliances, transportation costs and personal services) according to the quantity required for the average consumption habits of a European family of three. On this basis, Dublin was the eighth most expensive city in the world. Among the cheaper cities were London, Vienna, Madrid, Dusseldorf, New York, Chicago, Paris and Frankfurt.

The survey also looked at wage and salary levels, taking the gross wages of 12 different professions. Irish levels were comparatively low — 24th place in the sample of 52. Zürich had the highest wage and salary levels. But many popular destinations have higher pay than in Ireland, including Paris, Munich, Amsterdam and many other European cities.

Domestic purchasing power (in this case estimated simply by dividing the cost of the goods and services by the wages and salaries paid in each city) is far lower in Dublin than in most of Europe and in North America. Citizens of Los Angeles, Frankfurt, Zürich and Montreal enjoy the greatest purchasing power of all.

CHOOSING TO GO

While priorities vary, most people want to be sure of earning enough money to have a reasonable standard of living, enjoy life and save a little. Given that Dublin has been found to be the eighth most expensive city in the world (*above*), it is more than likely that you will be better off in money terms almost anywhere else, especially taking our punitive tax system into account.

13

Expectations or definitions of 'a reasonable standard of living' do vary and this is where Ireland is unable to compete. Even people who earn very well here cannot afford the kind of lifestyle that other workers in some countries, even those on low pay by that country's standards, take for granted.

Of course, there is that other intangible — quality of life — which should not be forgotten. People with experience of other countries hold Ireland high in this regard.

An Irish solution to an Irish problem: There are two problems which affect us all in this country: relative poverty and unemployment. Emigration often appears to be the only solution. We are all affected to some extent and everyone feels uneasy. Most unfairly, this unease finds its expression in criticism of people who leave, possibly partly because of jealousy on the part of people who stay, or a suspicion that they are rats abandoning a sinking ship. Politicians often foster this criticism, with references to the cost of education, especially third-level, and the importance of high direct taxation to keep the country going. There is little apparent recognition of the fact that for many, there is no real alternative but to leave. For others, the living standard and opportunities Ireland can provide bear no comparison to alternative destinations.

There is also a vague feeling we all have that each individual is duty-bound to contribute to the society in which we live. Some people have no chance of getting to make a contribution, even if they long to. The fact that life here is materially difficult, almost impossible, for some people, while others feel frustrated, helpless and totally unappreciated, poses some questions about our society and the way in which it is run.

The cost of providing an expensive, subsidised education for export is often thrown at the prospective emigrant, with good reason. The cost to Ireland of graduates who emigrate has been estimated at £87 million a year. That is £47 million in tuition and maintenance fees for vets, doctors, dentists, architects, engineers and other graduates, who then try their luck elsewhere, and £40 million for nurses, who obviously find many countries more willing to give them permanent jobs and adequate pay structures than their own. What has gone wrong?

Of course, if you cannot find a job reality is stark and the decision to leave simple; there is no element of real choice. You are doing everyone a favour by removing the embarrassment and guilt caused by your presence. Before you leave, it would be reasonable to expect someone to be able to tell you why you cannot find work here and what is the matter with a country which has, until recently, educated its 'most valuable resource' to a standard high enough to compete in any international marketplace.

The politicians do not seem to have any answers. They explain emigration away in terms of gaining valuable experience to bring home (which would be acceptable if there were openings to bring it back to), or suggest that some people are especially greedy and selfish to want more than they can earn here, or even present the ludicrous explanation that there isn't enough room for us all on this small island.

The emigrant's lament: Individuals will have to sort out for themselves the question of how much of a debt is owed to our society and what difference their taxes will make to health services, housing and education for the betterment of all. If you are cynical, this probably will not take very long. If you are unemployed, it will take no time at all.

It is worth recognising, however, that the future may not be all rosy. A decision to emigrate makes life easier for those at home, but is not necessarily a ticket to a wonderful future for the person going, no matter how well-paid the work may be. Emigration is a bit like an old movie — no one wants to look beyond the ride into the sunset.

Changing jobs and countries, never mind leaving the delights of home, is not easy regardless of your situation here. It is as well to be aware of the effect it can have on your personality. Emigrants are often not the happiest people in the world, especially Irish ones. Guilt — for abandoning family responsibilities, leaving the society that paid for your education to stew in its own juices, your failure to contribute to its development — can land on you later. So can loneliness, self-pity, bitterness about feeling forced to go and the failure of our society to appreciate you. These notions can combine with a strong sense of being an outsider in a foreign country, of not belonging to or understanding its culture, despite your efforts.

Add to this a gradual alienation from those at home and an insidious feeling that you must succeed — and it can all prove overpowering. After all, money is not everything and it is definitely *easier* to stay at home.

In the line of thinking that nothing could be as bad as your situation here, however, you are probably right. Our levels of unemployment and taxation are among the highest in the so-called developed world. There are hidden attributes though, that Ireland seems to develop at a distance.

'The shortest road to Tara is via Holyhead', as James Joyce observed. It is odd, but true, that Irish conversations overseas tend to be dominated by home. The inevitable comparisons between Ireland and the country in question are usually in Ireland's favour and there is always talk of going home at some stage, 'when things are better'. This strong desire to keep up the links must come from an attachment to the old sod that many of us do not know we possess and usually do not discover until there is a safe distance between us and it. Be ready for it and try to keep the rosy mist from your vision of the reality you left.

These statistics may help: the Department of Social Welfare now spends about £7 million a day on social welfare payments. In 1988, £2.5 billion was spent — one-third of government current expenditure. The number of social welfare claimants has almost doubled, from 20% of the population in 1966 to 37.4% in 1985. There are now over 1.3 million people dependent on social welfare payments. More than 1.2 million people live in serious poverty in Ireland today, according to the pre-budget submission of the Justice Commission of the Conference of Major Religious Superiors (Jan. 1989). At the end of December 1988, 18.7% of the workforce was unemployed (Central Statistics Office, 6 Jan. 1989), excluding those on training schemes for which one has to be unemployed to qualify. One in four people was earning less than £120 per week in 1986 (according to a 1988 ICTU report). Only about 15% of the population earns more than £15,500 a year (*Irish Times*, 9 Feb. 1989).

Emigration figures have increased rapidly in recent years, with an average of 15,000 a year between 1981 and 1986; 35,000 people emigrated in the 12 months up to 15 April 1988 (Central Statistics Office, 1 Feb. 1989). However, the difference between the number of people arriving and departing from Ireland in the same 12-month period was 73,000, implying that the real number emigrating could be over twice the official figure. The population of Ireland has fallen for the first time in 20 years, from 3,543,000 in

April 1987 to 3,538,000 in April 1988 (Central Statistics Office, 29 July 1988). This is despite the fact that we have the highest population growth rate in the EC (0.8%) and 33rd in the world (*World Bank Atlas*, 1988). We also have the second-lowest average life expectancy in the EC (74 years), shared with Luxembourg. Only the Portuguese can expect to die sooner (at 73 years)!

EUROPTIONS

There are endless choices and opportunities for Irish people in Europe. In many cases, it is simply a question of matching the right qualifications or skill with the right destination. The trick of finding work elsewhere is first to find out what is on offer and where. From that starting point you can decide what suits your purposes. You may also need to develop or adjust your skills to match the demand you have identified, or make sure your qualifications will be accepted.

It also helps to know something about visa requirements and systems of tax and social welfare, so that you can beat the bureaucracy — or at least be informed in your battle. The time spent on research should be worthwhile: it will help to give you a start and be ahead of the posse, with the right pieces of paper and the right skills to offer in the right place at the right time.

Finding out as much as you can before you go is the order of the day — who is going where, under what conditions and the reasons for their choice of destination. Make use of the experiences and hindsight of those who went before you. Circumstances and working environments change, demands change, but you are almost guaranteed that some strays from Ireland will already have branched down the path you are considering and something can always be learnt from their experiences.

You may also be choosing between several destinations. It is essential to find out as much as you can about their individual attractions and shortcomings before rushing into an option which may not be the best choice. Living standards, working conditions, taxation levels and the cost and availability of accommodation are all elements which should inform your decision.

What's in demand?: It is worth considering the places others have gone — not to follow blindly, but to get some idea of the general areas that are offering employment and the skills that are in demand. It stands to reason that demand for one area of work or training leads naturally to another, and that countries which are short of a particular skill may be short of others which are related. Today, in Europe, the international jobs market is looking for:

- computer personnel
- accountants
- architects
- financial services personnel
- electronic engineers and electronic technicians
- construction personnel (quantity surveyors, site managers, labourers, trades and craft people)
- civil engineers
- catering managers and catering supervisors
- mechanical (and production) engineers
- secretaries (especially bilingual)
- teachers of English as a foreign language (TEFL)
- marketing (and advertising/public relations) personnel
- management consultants (and systems analysts)
- nurses
- other medical or paramedical personnel, such as doctors, dentists, speech therapists and physiotherapists

Electronics, computer science or applications, and engineering — anyone with qualifications in these fields can easily command salaries far greater than they would receive at home. Irish training in these high-tech areas is very highly regarded in Europe and elsewhere. This is borne out by the statistics: 37% of the engineers graduating in 1986 found jobs overseas, or at least emigrated. It can be assumed that they were successful in their move by the increasing interest shown each year in final-year students by companies abroad. The majority of each year's crop is signed up by representatives of foreign companies or multinationals even before they qualify. For example, of the 27-member class of 1985 graduating in computer science in UCC, 8 went to jobs in Britain, 5 to West Germany, 4 to the Netherlands and 2 each to Switzerland and Japan. As the *Sunday Tribune* of 2 October 1988 reported, 'It was to Holland, and to Philips, that a few hundred of the best electronics engineers and computer scientists to come out of Irish colleges in the mid-1980s went. A BSc in computer systems from NIHE, Limerick, was among them. He went in April 1986 to see the facilities at Eindhoven, and returned along with 80 other fresh graduates later that year. Philips was recruiting heavily in Irish colleges in those years. They also recruited elsewhere because engineers could not be found in Holland in the numbers they wanted. Of the 36 in the BSc's department, only four were Dutch.'

Accountants and other 'financial' people, with an interest in currency trading, stockbroking, insurance, investment or merchant banking, will find opportunities. The financial services area is expanding rapidly, most notably in Britain but also in European financial centres. The planned Irish Financial Services Centre in Dublin is likely to provide opportunities with overseas companies, many of whom are currently training Irish personnel in preparation for operating here. Experience is not always necessary, since many companies offer in-service training, though a degree (in any discipline, but particularly business or commerce) helps and possibly a post-graduate qualification in business studies, economics or marketing.

Architects, civil engineers and all construction personnel are in demand; 57% of the architects graduating in 1986, for example, left Ireland for work elsewhere. This area must develop rapidly in the near future, as commercial and industrial sectors respond to the adjusting development demands of an unrestricted Europe. Major projects and infrastructural improvement will receive national and EC funding, and job opportunities are almost unlimited (as evidenced already by the Channel Tunnel project, road and rail programmes throughout the EC). At the moment, the construction industry is offering opportunities for surveyors and project managers, most notably in Britain and the Netherlands (and also in the Middle East), while the labouring end of the trade can find casual work relatively easily. Germany is still a popular destination.

The food science industry is booming and food scientists, production managers and indeed anyone with agricultural or horticultural qualifications can find opportunities. Though Europe is providing opportunities, Britain and the Middle East are also likely destinations. Veterinary surgeons are also guaranteed interesting experience and possibly better conditions than they would have at home. There is a shortage of vets throughout Europe: 46% of Irish vets emigrated as soon as they qualified in 1986.

Hotel and catering personnel can readily gain useful experience, especially qualified managers, since there is a strong demand for graduates in this area. Irish chefs and kitchen staff also have an excellent reputation internationally. But they are unlikely to find rates of pay and working conditions very much better than in Ireland. Travel within this industry is very much part of an overall career strategy and experience and training from respected institutions abroad widens the choices for the future. Switzerland, the world capital of hotel training, and France are popular destinations. With the increased movement of the business and commercial sector (as well as tourism) generated by the Single Europe Act, this area can only develop.

At the casual waitressing and barwork end of the scale, there are jobs everywhere for those experienced and efficient enough, though language problems and rates of pay may not compensate for the expense and difficulty of life in another country. Work can always be found, however, and it can be a good stand-by for the short-term while improving language and exploring options. Experience in this area is essential; many people are surprised by how difficult and demanding this work is and how little time a job lasts if they do not come up to scratch.

International marketing, advertising and public relations are work areas that are growing, especially in the unrestricted Europe context, as companies within the EC countries and outside   (such as Japan, South Korea and Scandinavia) take advantage of the new markets. It is possible to get into this area without specific professional qualifications and there are many short or post-graduate courses available. Your chances are enhanced by having a good knowledge of one or more European languages. Management consultancy is a related area and people with fluency in another language and a qualification in commerce, business studies or economics are much sought after.

Teachers are finding, more through force of circumstance than free choice, that it is relatively easy to find either casual work or permanent jobs with long-term contracts overseas. Both primary and secondary school teachers can now quite readily gain acceptance of their qualifications in many countries which, unlike Ireland, are short of teaching personnel. These are offering regular teaching jobs in State-recognised or academic institutions. At the moment, Britain and the USA are more fruitful work areas than most of Europe, though there are opportunities in Scandinavia and Switzerland. Times change, however, so keep informed of developments. Qualified teachers (or undergraduates intending to teach) who wish to improve their language capacity can take advantage of the language assistant schemes operated by various organisations in many European destinations. As the EC gets ready for 1992, there will be a greater emphasis on educational exchange between schools and language learning in the 12 countries. Teachers may find their skills more appreciated in other areas of EC cooperation, such as industrial language training and personnel exchange, as well as in youth exchange and intercultural experience programmes.

Many people, not only qualified teachers, find that a qualification in Teaching English as a Foreign Language (TEFL) is a ready passport for travel worldwide, although it may never earn them a fortune. Spain and Italy are among the most common destinations for jobs advertised here. For the more adventurous there are opportunities all over Europe, from Finland to Turkey.

People with good secretarial skills, especially word-processing, can travel easily. Their options are increased greatly if they are fluent in more than one European language, in particular German, Spanish and Italian. Those with commercial or business qualifications, as well as secretarial, will find themselves in great demand as businesses and organisations, taking advantage of the unrestricted market of the Single Europe Act, come to terms with the competition. Not only secretaries but linguists, too, will be needed for general purposes of translation, interpreting and interoffice communication between countries.

Short-term or temporary secretarial work is still easy to find almost everywhere. With a language, Europe is your oyster. All you have to do is sign on with agencies or advertise your services in English-language newspapers. Experience, good typing and familiarity with office equipment and procedure are very useful assets for anyone considering leaving for any destination.

Technical or practical skills are always in demand, though language can be a major barrier. Electricians, printers of all types and mechanics are most likely to find work. The vocational training and work-experience programmes run by FAS and other agencies (*see p. 30, 60*) provide openings for people with trades or practical skills to get experience of the European situation and language training in their area of work. Hairdressers and mechanics, for example, can move about quite easily and get casual work, not least because their skills are 'self-contained'.

Nurses and other medical personnel no longer suffer from difficulties with recognition of their Irish qualifications in a European context. However, language is a problem and Britain, the USA and the Middle East, as well as Australia, are more popular destinations — for obvious reasons. But there is a general shortage of nurses in the EC and other medical skills, such as radiography and physiotherapy, are often in demand in non-EC European countries. More than 2400 Irish nurses left Ireland during 1988, as did a similar number in 1987.

FINDING THE DEMAND

Employers and agencies all over the world have realised that there is a highly qualified and trained workforce in Ireland — and severe economic problems. We have become one of the first targets in any recruiting campaign.

Shortages of trained personnel in a particular work area occur from time to time in every country, leaving the field wide-open for the applicant from overseas. Often the demand is met quickly, as local training authorities rush to comply with employers' changing needs or as a cheaper labour supply, possibly of another nationality, becomes available. In the meantime, companies and agencies will advertise overseas and sometimes immigration restrictions will be relaxed while the gap is filled.

It is important to keep up to date with developments and trends in your particular work area. For example, the new locations of operations of major multinationals, State investment in new hospital or educational facilities, development of holiday resorts or major building programmes — all create specific demands. EC-funded development is also evident in many areas in the run-up to 1992.

Subscription to a professional or trade magazine, membership of any work-related or professional organisations and attendance at the 'open days' and latter-day 'hiring fairs' run by potential employers at many third-level colleges (and by international recruiting agencies in hotels) are all useful for possible destination ideas. Also, keep a weather eye on newspaper advertisements.

WHAT YOU NEED

A language and a skill: An obvious, but useful point to remember when deciding where to go is that the person who can communicate most readily will get the job before the possibly more skilled and experienced person who cannot speak the language. Similarly, people with specific skills to sell — whether technical, secretarial, mechanical or professional — and qualifications on paper to prove it will find better paid work, more easily, than those who can only settle for unskilled jobs where they are competing with a greater number of applicants, most of whom will have the advantage of local knowledge and languages, and fewer living expenses than the outsider.

The possession of a professional or trade qualification makes life easier, not least because your job-search has an obvious direction and starting point, though you may have no desire to stay with the same kind of work once you become established and more aware of local opportunities.

The only possible stumbling block (easily researched from the relevant authority either in Ireland or in the host country, or your union or professional association) is whether your qualification is recognised as equivalent to that held by locals in your field. If it is not, you may have to take an examination and/or follow a course in the other country in order to practise or register as a member of that trade or professional organisation.

Cooperation by EC member states in the recognition of professional qualifications is being encouraged by the authorities at the moment. The free movement of workers between EC countries should become much easier in the few years preceding 1992 (*see p. 65*).

Accountants and engineers appear more likely to suffer from restrictions and difficulties with registration and recognition of qualifications than other professionals. Of the trades, electricians and plumbers are most likely to have difficulties with official licensing systems.

No Qualifications?: It is possible to capitalise on the high regard in which Irish qualifications are held in many countries even if you lack a long-term professional or technical qualification. Obviously the better your training, the easier your search for an interesting position. It is true, however, that people can sell themselves short. The art of persuading someone to take you on can be far more useful than any amount of professional qualifications. If you can convince an employer that you are the person he needs, and are confident and impressive enough, then your bluff may be called and a chance offered to prove your worth. People seem to get what they give the impression they deserve, so set your sights as high as possible initially and, while no one will take you on as managing director, you can at least try for an area in which there are chances of movement upwards, once you have proved yourself and gained experience. A dead-end job, taken on just to tide you over, has a terrible tendency to become a permanent engagement; as you get used to it, your horizons narrow and you never have time anyway to look for something better.

It is a fatal mistake to represent or advertise yourself as willing or capable of doing almost anything. You lose by not appearing to have any of the specific skills needed for a particular job and your energy is wasted in chasing after all kinds of dead ends. The effect on you, and on potential employers, is that of the archetypal jack-of-all-trades and master-of-none.

The situation in Ireland is far more demanding in terms of qualifications than in many countries; it is a symptom of our comparatively highly educated workforce and our economic problems. Elsewhere, initiative and brashness are admired and even expected of an interviewee. There is less immediate likelihood of being laughed out of the office if you present yourself for a job without the stipulated requirements.

Depending on your interests and destination, a short course (even a FAS scheme or a local nightclass) could be presented, with imagination, as suitable preparation for a specific job, especially if you have other assets, such as experience of a related area or a number of useful skills. Here at least is one situation in which the outsider has the advantage and a greater chance of presenting previous experience and training in a favourable light. Most potential employers overseas are still quite unfamiliar with the names of Irish institutions and with what is highly regarded in our education and training.

The depth or quality of your knowledge may not be as important as the label and status it gives you, which will make your job-hunt more specific and then provide genuine useful experience to market for future moves in the same area. Among

the short courses available which will rarely prove a waste of time
are:

- wordprocessing
- typing
- bookkeeping or office procedure
- teaching English as a foreign language (TEFL)
- translation (if you already have a second language)
- sales and marketing
- basic accountancy
- computer operating/basic programming

Proof that you have completed a course is important. If certificates
or diplomas are not issued, make sure to get an official letter from
the institution involved, stating your name, title of course and its
length.

Any other talents you possess and have completed courses in
may also be exploitable. While of little value alone, they serve as
evidence to back-up character and personality claims and may be
useful for giving casual private tuition. Examples are dramatic,
artistic or musical awards, life-saving, first-aid, gymnastic or
sailing qualifications.

WHO'LL LET YOU IN?

Current immigration policies: At the moment the real problem is
not finding a job elsewhere, but who will let you in. Apart from
the countries of the EC, which must provide (in theory at least)
complete freedom of access to individual members for working
within the Community, Europe remains rather a closed shop.
Beating the system requires some research and ingenuity, as well
as a basic understanding of immigration policy. The same general
policy applies worldwide, not only for non-EC Europe, but also
for the USA, Canada, Australia and the Far East.

Jobs for foreigners are not exactly a priority of most countries,
many of which are hardpressed at the moment to find work for
their own people — unless they are suffering the kind of specific
shortages mentioned above. If that is the case, restrictions will be
relaxed for people with the particular skill or qualification
required. Otherwise, without those need-dictated exemptions,
immigration policy usually has an indigenous bias, insisting that

employers must demonstrate that a specific post needs specific skills and qualifications, or experience and personal qualities, that cannot be found within their own country. To do this often requires advertising the post within the country and even conducting interviews. No matter how special you are, it is highly unlikely that there is no other person in an entire population who is not also suitable for the job in question. The onus is on the employer to prove that this is so or that he has made at least a reasonable effort to make sure, before you can be formally offered a job and issued a visa. One approach is to try to find work first, having entered the country for a short-term visit.

Getting in from the inside: While you might have no difficulty finding an employer on the spot who would be glad, even delighted to take you on (as can be the case in Sweden, Norway, Switzerland and to a lesser extent Austria and Finland), few employers are prepared to go through the exacting procedures required of them. They may complain of the crazy immigration policy, but it is up to them to regularise their position *and* yours by obtaining a work visa, migration permit or whatever the system is. Most immigration departments dislike and discourage employers from trying to regularise people who have come to them on spec, unofficially, while visiting the country as a tourist or on a visitor's visa — because they are trying to work backwards through the system, for one thing, and bureaucracy hates any disruption to its processes. They also fear word might spread that this approach is possible.

One way they discourage this kind of 'backdoor entry' is by accepting working visa applications only from *outside* the country, so even if you have managed to bypass the system in the first place, you have to start again, in the right order.

Almost all countries demand that the prospective employee makes application, with the help of his future boss, from outside the country. It is expensive and time-consuming, even if you do not have to return to your country of origin but can apply from the nearest foreign capital, as is often the case. That said, it is sometimes possible to go about getting a working visa from within and not all countries make you leave first.

Illegality: Unless you are lucky, you are unlikely to get very far on a tourist visa. More questions are asked in some countries than in others. If you change your status unofficially, having entered the country as a short-term visitor or holiday-maker, it will usually be illegal. It is a general, but valid rule of job-hunting that it is the decent employers who will not break the law by taking you on illegally. The less said about the others the better.

It is also a general rule that most countries catch up with illegal workers eventually; the heartache you go through and the conditions you work and live under while trying to avoid this are not usually compensated by the pay your weak position dictates. Illegal work is insecure, difficult and prone to exploitation. It makes more sense to find an employer who is prepared to regularise you; he will then have obligations to protect you with social insurance and other cover.

Paving your way: Of course, there is nothing to stop you writing on spec to companies in countries which have tough immigration requirements — you could be pleasantly surprised by the response. If you have a particular skill which is in short supply in, for example, Switzerland or Sweden, there is a chance of finding someone who would be prepared to go through the whole procedure of sponsoring your migration. Some may even offer travel and relocation allowances. It is a long shot, but worth trying. Ignore the official embassy line on the almost absolute impossibility of getting a visa ('We have unemployment problems of our own', etc) and write directly to prospective employers, having done your homework on what is needed, where. The visa situation could change drastically if you have a specific job offer.

THE JOB-SEARCH

Some approaches: There is a systematic way to approach the whole matter of persuading someone to employ you in Europe. As with so many aspects of life in Ireland, it is often a question of who you know. Familiarity with, or at least knowledge of, the right people (or agencies) is important, for getting to hear about opportunities first — or at all.

Many recruitment programmes, even for EC-funded schemes, as well as individual positions, are conducted and filled without much publicity or advertising. Contacts, awareness of developments in your field and an ear to the ground are essential.

The careers departments of any third-level institutions, especially universities, are a good source of general information for the professionally trained on who's recruiting where; these offices are often accessible for discreet enquiry by those not officially on the books. Public libraries, local Community Information Centres and FAS can tell you about organised programmes (*see also below*).

If you are employed, look within your own organisation, both for possibilities of specific jobs and any overseas contacts the company may have. Personal recommendations and contacts go a long way when breaking into a new environment.

Look also at the big Irish companies with business divisions outside the country and at the multinationals which operate here. There are a number of multinational companies which could provide opportunities for those on their staff, or possible contacts elsewhere to the outsider. Over 300 electronics companies from North America, Europe and the Far East operate in Ireland, not to mention the many chemical and pharmaceutical firms. Many large companies in the food, drink or consumer goods trade, such as Irish Distillers, have marketing staff and sales personnel all over the world. PARC, the management and recruitment division of Aer Lingus, is another example of a company which recruits here for its worldwide operations. If you can manage to get any post in such an organisation and are prepared to invest some time, opportunities overseas may prove more accessible and attractively packaged for the person on the inside.

Keeping an eye on newspaper advertisements is an obvious step towards finding a job abroad. It is surprisingly easy to forget about or miss the one vital issue that advertised the job of your dreams. The newspapers each Sunday carry a range of advertisements. The *Sunday Press* is especially good on jobs overseas, particularly for medical personnel. The *Sunday Tribune* and the *Irish Times* (Fridays) carry high-tech, computing and electronics ads as well as accountancy ads. For teachers, *The Guardian* (Tuesdays) and *The Times' Educational Supplement* (Fridays) are an essential adjunct to Thursday's *Irish Independent*. And don't forget the evening papers — sales jobs, TEFL and all sorts of odd work comes up in the small ads.

Signing-on with at least one recruitment agency in Ireland is another obvious step. Among the agencies here that recruit staff for international contracts are (*addresses listed on p. 114*):

- **European Employment Consultants (EEC):** for management and professional personnel, bilingual secretaries, general manufacturing, chemicals, personnel management and human resources sectors; interested in graduates with good language skills, especially German.
- **Santos Engineering Services:** for building construction personnel, water supply, roads, ports and process plants on a variety of international projects.
- **O'Grady Peyton International:** mostly medical staff but also teachers for the Middle East.
- **PARC Recruitment Consultants:** for managerial and medical staff, short-term contracts included; they run the Ibn al Bitar hospital in Baghdad, among others.
- **The Accountants Panel.**
- **CSR Consultants:** for computing jobs.
- **Head Hunt International:** for secretarial, accountancy, engineering, electronics, computer and sales and marketing posts.
- **CCM Recruitment International:** for nurses.
- **Worldwide Recruitment Ltd:** for trades personnel, on-site staff and people in the building trade in general.

It is also well worth signing on with a UK agency in your field. They are likely to have a wider choice of destinations and good packages. All of these agencies have offices in London (*see addresses, p. 115*).

- **Lansdowne International Services** and **International Training and Recruitment Link** are two large general companies that specialise in the international market with divisions for different work areas.
- **Elan Computing** and **Skilled Compupeople** are self-explanatory examples of the many companies which deal with vacancies worldwide.
- **The British Council** and **Gabbitas Truman Thring** both provide useful information for teachers.

You should also consider the aid programmes run by State development agencies, Government agencies or diplomatic posts. Who knows? You could end up promoting the 'Young Europeans' for the IDA or selling holidays in Ireland to the Americans —

somebody has to. Don't forget either that voluntary service and workcamp organisations, both here and in Britain, can provide a means of visiting countries with strict visa requirements, if you are prepared to work for nothing or simply cover your expenses:

- APSO (Agency for Personal Service Overseas) is the umbrella organisation for aid workers.
- VSI (Voluntary Service International) is an organisation which offers voluntary work placements.
- Comhcairdeas (the Irish Workcamp movement).
- Projects organised by the World Bank and United Nations.
- The Development Cooperation Division of the Department of Foreign Affairs advertises interesting posts for the well-qualified from time to time, although most projects are in the Third World.

Organised schemes and work-exchange programmes: It is often easier to move between European countries under the auspices of an organised programme. There are lots of groups which run schemes, many of them oriented to work experience (*see addresses, p. 112*). Some organisations aim to promote intercultural understanding; others aim to improve an individual's concrete skills, such as language capacity or vocational training; still others aim to provide experience of the workplace on an international basis. Details for specific EC programmes are given on pp. 60-63.

- **FAS (Foras Áiseanna Saothair),** Ireland's National Training and Employment Authority coordinates many schemes. The Sponsorship Section of FAS organises long-stay training and work-experience programmes in foreign companies for new graduates. The scheme operates all over the world. Principal destinations in Europe are Germany, the Netherlands, Spain, Portugal, Sweden, Denmark and Switzerland. (People also go to Japan, Hong Kong, South Korea and North America on this programme.) It is largely for technical or technologically trained people, though 20% of the participants have non-technical qualifications, such as marketing diplomas. The average length of stay is 2 years, but some stay with the overseas company for as long as 5 years.

A series of talks is organised by FAS on this programme to final-year students in October or November each year. It is growing rapidly — in 1988 more than 82 took part.

- **The Young Workers Exchange Programme** provides work experience in EC countries, administered by FAS and the YEB (Youth Exchange Bureau, *see p. 61*).
- **The Irish Department of Labour** organises the 'stage' or trainee work experience programme, which is conducted according to agreements with a number of countries. The trainees, or 'stagiares' (usually aged between 18 and 30) can spend a year getting work experience elsewhere, having completed their vocational training in Ireland. Many of the countries which issue work visas to 'stagiares' are otherwise quite inaccessible to foreign workers. The YEB and other agencies also administer similar programmes.
- **The YEB-administered International Fund for Ireland's Wider Horizons programme** and **AFS—Interculture Ireland's Young Worker Programme** offer travel, vocational experience and develop international understanding.
- **The International Association for the Exchange of Students for Technical Experience (IAESTE)** offers long-term placements usually, but not always, through colleges in 48 countries. They also have summer placements, of between one and three months during May to October, to destinations which are difficult to get into independently, such as Finland.
- **The International Association for Students of Economics and Management (AIESEC)** is a similar organisation to that mentioned above, but rather less accessible. It is intended for those with business and commerce qualifications.

It must be stressed that there are lots of funded, organised schemes — those mentioned above are only a sample. Even an organisation as esoteric as the Royal Irish Academy (RIA) has annual exchange programmes, most notably with Austria. There is sure to be something suitable for you, if you are prepared to be part of an organised supervised scheme. Such a route can provide an excellent starting point for the person who wants to find work in Europe — and it helps that someone will pay you to do so.

WHAT TO BRING

The rule for any travel or move is to take as little as possible. The chances of losing precious possessions and enduring hassles with transportation are then lessened. Ease of movement is everything, especially when your final destination is uncertain or the clothing and equipment necessary for the lifestyle of your future work-place may be very different from expectations. It is a safe bet that anything you need to live comfortably in the same style as everyone else at your destination will be available locally, though prices may differ considerably.

There are some personal papers that are almost universally useful, even essential, for dealing with either job-hunting or local bureaucracy. They should not be forgotten — replacement or having them sent on will be troublesome, risky and cause delays.

One way of keeping precious original documents clean and presentable while travelling is to roll them together in a poster tube, which is easier to keep an eye on. Anything packed flat, even in folders, gets surprisingly dog-eared in the average suitcase.

CHECKLIST

- **Clothes:** To save time and extra expense in the early days, bring at least one outfit suitable for attending interviews, and two sets of working clothes. Shoes and underwear are probably cheaper and easier to buy before you go.

- **Personal papers:** Any or all of the following may be required at some time. It is easier to have them with you.
  - birth certificate (full version)
  - vaccination certificates
  - prescription for glasses or contact lenses
  - prescription for and generic names of any special medication you may need

- insurance policy number
- social insurance (PRSI) number
- statements of Irish bank accounts and their numbers
- identity cards from any college or workplace. These can be useful as back-up to establish your *bona fides* and less risky to carry at all times than your passport.
- union membership cards and those from any work-related association or organisation
- private health insurance policy (VHI) and information stating entitlements under health insurance schemes in countries where they have reciprocal arrangements
- ISIC (International Student Identity Card) for those who qualify (possible to obtain one on enrolment in an educational institute or language school overseas).
- Youth Hostel Association (YHA) membership is useful and available for people of any age. It is often cheaper in other countries since rates are lower for visitors' membership.

- **Work papers:** While you may be unwilling to risk losing your precious degree or diploma, it is almost essential to carry original documents. Photocopies are treated with great suspicion in many countries and while it is useful to have some with you to leave with potential employers, the original should be available for inspection. A way round this is to have good quality copies made before you leave and have them stamped and signed by the issuing body. Work references could also be certified in this way. Translations should be prepared before you leave. Bring any of the following which apply to you:
  - original or certified copy of degree or diploma
  - certificates related to training
  - certificates related to leisure pursuits and interests
  - originals and copies of work references
  - leaving certificate (or final school exam certificate)
  - references or names and phone numbers of referees from training or educational institutions
  - up to date curriculum vitae (perhaps with space left to add future address and phone number).

2
Things to Consider

SALARIES AND THE COST OF LIVING

There are two major elements involved when choosing a destination — domestic purchasing power and the strength and stability of the currency in which you are being paid on international exchange markets.

Domestic purchasing power is vital: it refers to how far your money goes or what you can buy for what you earn in the country where you are working. This will dictate your standard of living and what you can save.

The second element (relative currency value in exchange) is only important if you intend to leave the country and exchange what you have saved in the currency of your pay packet into another currency.

Of course, these two elements are linked: places with low living costs rarely have currency with high value in exchange. The opposite, though, is not necessarily always the case. Pay levels should, but do not always, reflect these factors.

When you take the quality of life and your enjoyment of the location into account as well as economic considerations, your decision may alter. (After all, many of us think that Dublin would be a great place to live in, if only you had enough money — and perhaps more sunshine.) The bottom line is, therefore, that you cannot assume that somewhere with high pay will necessarily provide the best option.

Take, for example, living and working in Sweden with payment in the local currency, the Swedish krone, in comparison to living and working in Greece with payment in Greek drachmas. The cost of living in Greece is comparatively low: food, clothes and entertainment all cost less than they would here, though inflation is growing. To have a reasonable lifestyle there, you do not have to spend a lot and pay levels necessarily reflect this — salaries are comparatively low. It is correspondingly difficult to save what is left over out of your pay packet. Recent economic factors, notably inflation and EC membership, have also reduced the drachma's strength on the international exchange. Its value is unstable and steadily decreasing. When you go to exchange your savings on leaving the country, you do not get very many US dollars, Irish pounds or whatever. So, although it is not expensive to live in Greece, your savings are hard-won and of relatively little value outside the country. This is regardless of your estimation of the quality of life there.

The cost of living in Sweden is astronomical, even by Irish standards. Taxation and social security payments take up a large portion (over 40%) of the average wage. Wages are also high and Swedish residents have an excellent standard of living in material terms. Food, clothing, drink and entertainment cost around 30% to 50% more than they do in Ireland. Therefore, you need to earn around three times as much as you do here to have a reasonable lifestyle and it is correspondingly difficult to save.

Obviously, the second factor, strength of the relevant currency in exchange, is most relevant to your destination. If you are going somewhere 'unpleasant' for a short period of intense hard work — a German pickle factory, for example — with the express intention of saving a lump sum, the position of the currency in which you are paid is vital. On the other hand, if you are settling for good or simply want to enjoy the experience of life in Greece, for example, it does not matter.

Wherever you are going, there is no point in simply mentally translating the wage mentioned into Irish currency. It either (deceptively) sounds like a small fortune and you then assume that the same small fortune would purchase the same amount of goodies that it would at home, or it seems like a pittance and you forget that things might be cheaper where people earn so little. Places with high salaries do, unfortunately, usually have living costs to match, because people have to be paid higher wages, by our standards, to live 'normally'.

RELATIVE LIVING COSTS AND WAGES

As a general rule of thumb, wages and living costs are high in Scandinavia and Northern Europe, average in Britain and European countries such as France, the Netherlands and Germany, and low in the Mediterranean region. This is a very rough guide and completely ignores the other major factor which will affect your pay packet — relative levels of taxation (*below*).

There are some professions, such as nursing, engineering or computer science, which are in constant demand. In these cases, local conditions vary as the market is flooded or alternative labour supplies found. Currencies also fluctuate. It is vital to do some research into recent pay and working and living conditions in different countries before choosing your destination. The quality of a particular work situation can change very quickly, often for the worse. It is easy to be influenced by hyped-up advertisements or destinations which were popular with former colleagues and to forget the extent to which you can pick and choose.

For more information on the current financial scene in Europe, banks in many countries publish surveys of the cost of living. The *Daily Telegraph's* guide to working and living overseas, called *Working Abroad*, gives a detailed examination of the financial position of the expatriate worker in many popular destinations, including most European countries. It is aimed very much at the executive with a high salary and lifestyle to match. The sum it says a single person in Paris needs just to cover living costs at 'a moderate executive level' is nearly three times the total pay an Irish secretary could live on and save from in the same city three years ago.

EUROPEAN TAXATION

Income tax is a very complicated business as we all know, often to our cost. The individual case frequently bears no relation to the general rule. Throughout Europe, rules and regulations vary widely. This is also true within the increasingly standardised unit of the EC where, not surprisingly, the European Commission has not yet attempted to open, yet alone unravel, the can of worms that the current tax systems of the twelve countries represent.

These few pages deal with aspects of direct taxation in Europe in general. They can only draw your attention to the existence of such things as residency requirements and double-taxation agreements. The tax position within the EC is outlined on pp. 49-51 and more specific details and information sources are given under the individual countries' entries (*see pp. 67-93*).

Most of us are happily ignorant about such things and would rather stay that way. Unfortunately, they have a nasty habit of creeping up on you at times and in places where you least expect to be hit by the taxman. Few of these issues are straightforward, so professional help from accountants or tax advisers is definitely recommended. Your local friendly bank manager may be able to advise you. Failing that, buy a good tax guide. These pages can only introduce you to the whole sorry subject.

PAYE: The pay-as-you-earn system is operated by most countries in Europe. This is where the employer makes deductions from each payment of your wage or salary according to official income bands and allowances on the basis of a tax certificate, which is prepared for each individual by the central tax authority of the country in question. Total projected earnings (for that tax year) are taken into account on the basis of your first job or jobs, as well as your income from other sources (such as property, savings or investments). The rate of social insurance you must pay and the various personal allowances and reliefs available to you are also decided. Without a tax certificate, the employer may be able to make deductions according to his own estimate of your liability, or the maximum amount ('emergency' tax) may be deducted.

It is important to get the tax certificate sorted out as quickly as possible, as over- or under-payment may have to wait for the end of the tax year rather than be simply adjusted in future pay packets. Remember, too, the income tax year and the calendar year are not the same thing — and different countries start their tax years from different dates.

Tax-free allowances: All humane countries which operate a PAYE system allow people to earn a certain amount before they are liable for income tax. Income from other sources (investments, property, etc) is taken into account, but this is not usually a problem for someone from another country who has little with him apart from personal possessions.

The tax-free personal allowance is usually around 20% of the average wage, more in countries which have high living costs. Therefore, in theory, someone who does not exceed the personal allowance (as may happen when only working for a short time) should not have to pay any tax. However, the way in which PAYE systems operate prevents this seemingly simple outcome. The general rule is to deduct first and, if necessary, refund later. There can be long delays even if you are entitled to a rebate.

Projected income and residency: Your tax-free allowances and other deductions (for dependants, expenses, etc) are given on the basis that you are a fully involved member of that society, living in it for a long time and therefore entitled to whatever little let-outs and non-taxed perks that country gives its residents. Problems arise when you do not actually stay long enough to be considered resident and therefore your tax-free allowance and other allowances are not given.

A tax office's definition of residency has nothing to do with residence permits or other bureaucracy. Since residence is usually decided on the basis of a tax year rather than a calendar year, the date on which you start work could be important. You might be living in the country long enough to apply for a rebate on the first lot of tax you paid at the end of the tax year, even if you are not going to be resident for a full calendar year. Alternatively, you might be able to claim that you are staying indefinitely and the country in question is your usual place of abode, if you have been there for more than six months of a fiscal (tax) year and can give a local address for correspondence — rather than that at which you actually reside in another country. This claim, of course, also depends on the length and type of your visa, but tax offices in many countries do not communicate efficiently with immigration departments.

Usually there is some subclause somewhere within the tortuous wording of the tax form, or a date for application with which you cannot comply, that ensures you do not get any money back. Indeed, if your tax has been deducted on the basis of having the allowances of an ordinary or permanent resident (from the time the job began or whenever you were taken off emergency tax), you could well end up owing the tax office money. It is possible to claim rebates, either in the country in question or when you get home, but tax offices are similar the world over — notoriously reluctant to part with money. Once it is in their possession, it tends to stay there.

Rebates: The reason why you may not see any money for a long time, if ever, is the rebate system. Many countries will not accept rebate applications until the end of the tax year in question, when they like people to complete tax returns. This effectively precludes you from claiming a rebate if you are not on the spot to complete a tax return. It may be possible to complete a rebate application when you are leaving and give a forwarding address. If not, double-taxation agreements, which Ireland has with many countries, provide a means whereby tax paid abroad can be credited as though you had paid it in your own country and, by extension, overpayment can be refunded. It is possible, but difficult, to claim here for overpayment elsewhere. For one thing, you may find yourself being asked too many searching questions about your exact income and savings, both here and in the country in question. Even if you are entitled to a rebate, it will be very slow to arrive, often at least one fiscal year later for the host country.

Going away and coming home: People leaving jobs in Ireland to go abroad are usually entitled to a full-year's allowances here, if they leave before the end of the tax year. This could qualify them for a refund. It seems that you can qualify by offsetting a full-year's tax allowances against your earnings of the partial year, that is, the amount you have earned since the beginning of the tax year on 6th April. Until recently, you were only allowed a half-year's allowances. If you are going away and will be out of the country for at least one full tax year, then you should tell the tax office here before you go and give them your P45 form (from the employer you are leaving). They will send the refund to your forwarding address outside the country.

Be careful about the tax office here when you come home. If you stay away long enough and seem to intend to go away again, they can declare you non-resident here, too, and remove your tax-free allowances. You will then pay tax on your full income here until you requalify. Normally though, people are entitled to a full-year's allowances when they return, even though they may only work for part of that year. It is well worth timing your return for the middle of the year to maximise the benefit of this. Your savings, or earnings from overseas, will also be liable to tax here if you do not stay away for long enough, usually one full year.

Many banks and building societies offer deposit accounts which are free of tax deducted at source for the overseas investor. A minimum period away is required. All interest is credited gross, sometimes at a higher rate. Such facilities are worth finding out about before you go, if you intend leaving money on deposit here.

3
The EC:
Rules and Regulations

As a citizen of a Community country, you are entitled to do a paid job, work independently, or set up a business in another EC country. Your wife or your husband, and also your children, are likewise free to work in the country where you take up residence. However, in the case of Greece, which has been a member of the community since 1981, and Portugal and Spain, who joined in 1986, the free movement of workers will not be effective until 1988 (Greece and 1993 (Portugal and Spain).

Europeans, you have rights
official booklet published by the Commission of the
European Communities, Luxembourg, 1987

AN 'OPEN' EUROPE?

The completely free movement of people, goods and services throughout the EC should exist by 1992, under the terms of the Single Europe Act which came into force in 1987. But, in practice, an open Europe is still a long way off. For the hopeful worker, with passport ready and sights set on the wonderful opportunities that exist elsewhere in the EC, there are still regulations to get tied up in and barriers to overcome. Language ability is the most obvious barrier, but there is also a certain amount of red tape.

While, in theory, any EC national is free to work or study in any member state, the reality is dictated by that individual's language capacity, financial solvency and ability to deal with tiresome bureaucracy. Where there is a country which may provide a job, there is paperwork to complete with conditions to fulfil. The conditions are not difficult, but it helps if you have money, speak the language and understand the rules.

The difference between ideal theory and actual complex reality is obvious from the EC's booklet, *Europeans, you have rights*. This tells you about those rights in wonderful, short, simple statements, with all the weight of the European Commission's authority and Community ideals of unity. Then, in a long series of tortuous subclauses, each beginning '*However ...*', they tell you about official limits of those rights or the exact conditions you must fulfil to attain them. They do suggest going to the European Court if you do not manage to get satisfaction, but that drastic step is only for cases of discrimination beyond the officially acceptable conditions and restrictions. Some of the exceptions and limitations apply only to the more recent members (Spain, Portugal and Greece) which, in many areas of work and social welfare, will not have the same regulations until 1993.

It surprises many of us that there is no chance of simply taking off. You cannot go to live in another European country, free as a bird and just because you feel like it. You cannot avoid having to answer questions or explain yourself to someone. You cannot expect to find somewhere sunnier and continue to live in the same circumstances as you do here, whether it is on the dole or not, without obeying the red tape and conforming to requirements.

The image of a Europe without barriers is strictly for the real birds and the advertising campaigns. Each country is entitled to enquire into your circumstances and your reasons for staying, and put you through some kind of official verification process. The countries of the European Community like 'aliens' to have a name, address and telephone number; they are even happier if 'aliens' have an identity card with them at all times. If Europe is our shared playground and industrial estate, it is one with strict pollution rules, tagged and wing-clipped birds and some very fussy neighbours.

WORKING LEGALLY IN THE EC

*You can travel to another country of the European Community with your identity card or passport, without any formalities, provided you do not intend to work. **However** [author's emphasis], if you wish to stay for a long time, you must have a particular reason for this, either because you are working there or are looking for work or because you are married and entitled to live there, or because of your family or personal situation (eg you are the father or mother of a migrant worker). Minors (children under the age of 18 in the majority of member states) require their parents' written consent to cross a border.*

This quote from *Europeans, you have rights* tells us that, while you can travel freely throughout the EC if you have a valid passport, the situation changes if you intend to work or to stay anywhere for longer than the average holiday time. Three months is the general cut-off point. But many countries require you to go through some form of identity registration almost as soon as you arrive, if you intend to stay.

Identity registration: Many of our European neighbours operate a national registration system by which they keep tabs on the identities and movements of all their residents, both nationals and non-nationals (or 'aliens'). Personal details (such as name, address, nationality and birthdate) are recorded in a central filing system and sometimes an identity card is issued. You are required to undergo this process at the police station, aliens' office or municipal authority (town hall) nearest your place of residence in the country in question.

In many cases, identity registration is merely a formality intended only for people who are staying for longer than three months. Tourists are not really expected to take it upon themselves to register, since their personal details are recorded automatically in tourist accommodation.

However, if you intend to stay in the country for longer than three months, or to work at any stage (either during those three months or for a longer period), identity registration is necessary. The problem with this is that in most countries, you are expected to register within three to eight days of arrival. Registration is then linked to getting a valid residence permit (and in the case of Denmark, medical care and a bank account) for which you often need to have a job. Therefore, although you can stay with 'no restrictions' in any EC country, working or not, for three months, you are really expected to have work almost immediately or a definite job offer in order to comply with the formalities of identity registration.

In Belgium, for example, according to the official *Young Visitors Guide*, 'All foreigners must, within eight working days of their arrival, register with the municipal authorities of their place of residence so that their particulars may be placed on the Foreigners' Register.' EC citizens will receive an 'attestation d'immatriculation modèle B' (registration certificate type B). The period covered by this document will depend on the 'period of business' of the applicant. It is unclear as to what happens to those who have not yet found a job and, therefore, have no definite 'period of business'.

According to the Danish Embassy in Ireland, 'If you intend to stay [in Denmark] for a period of three months or more, you are liable to notify the Local National Register [Folkeregisteret] of your arrival not later than five days after arrival. When the National Register has been notified, you will automatically be included in the general health insurance scheme.' However, in order to register with the Danish Folkeregisteret and get a personal code number certificate (essential for all dealings with the authorities, to get a medical card and to open a bank account), you have to have a valid residence/labour permit — for which you need written details of a specific job offer.

There, therefore, appears to be a direct conflict between being entitled (as a citizen of an EC member state) to stay for up to three months in any EC country in order to look for work and the identity registration requirements of many member states. Although their status should be the same, a distinction is made in many countries between tourists, those who are seeking employment and those who actually have a job offer. This distinction becomes operative in the first eight days — not at the end of the initial three-month period.

It seems rather bureaucratic, even Big Brotherish, in our supposedly unrestricted, free-moving Europe to expect people to declare their intentions of staying longer than three months before even the first week is up. It could easily be argued later that you had not intended to stay but changed your mind, having taken some time to settle in and investigate the possibilities. How can anyone read another person's mind and see there the different intentions — either a three-month holiday or a three-month period spent looking for work? And, having been told, what difference does it make to the country anyway? The logic of requiring immediate identity registration is hard to follow.

Of course, many people blithely stay and even work for ages without even being aware of the requirements. Some countries are far stickier about following the regulations than others. In this book, the 'official line' is presented and the individual can choose how far to follow it. It is worth remembering that the chances of changing your status and getting the vital residence permit increase the more you do it 'by the book' from the word go.

Remember, too, that registration of aliens often happens automatically, without your knowledge, when you stay in an hostel, hotel or any form of commercial accommodation, even a campsite.

Residence permits: There is an official time limit of three months on your stay in most EC countries, whether you are on holiday, travelling, studying or looking for work. Then, you have to 'regularise' your position. In practice, this usually means either starting a job or a course of study in order to qualify for a residence permit — or going home. You are expected not only to register (*above*), but also to obtain an official permit to continue residence. The name and official requirements for this permit vary from EC country to country. Most like to call it a 'residence' permit and use the same system for intending workers and students. In all cases, your financial situation is taken into account.

Even if you are looking for work, and take some time to find it, you can still only stay for three months in another EC country. Even those three months carry restrictions, since you have to be able to support yourself and be prepared, if necessary, to provide proof that you have the resources to live 'without imposing a financial burden on the country concerned'. Unfortunately, it can take months to transfer the unemployment benefit to which you were entitled at home and which you could reasonably expect to be able to use in your job hunt. If your circumstances (especially financial, but also possibly your lifestyle) do not meet with approval, you can be refused permission to stay.

Thus, while EC members are free to live and work in other countries, they are not encouraged to settle if it is likely that they will be a drain on the resources of the country concerned. No EC member state wants to lengthen its own dole queue or suffer increased local competition from other countries' job-seekers.

In theory, you are expected to have a job, or at least a definite offer, before you can apply for a residence permit. In practice, however, you need to have a residence permit before many employers will consider you for any good long-term job. You also (usually) need to get a residence permit as soon as you begin working, whether you have been in the country for less than three months or not.

With employment, you can stay as long as either the job or the residence permit lasts. This is usually geared to coincide. But a permit for one year or five years can be issued on the basis of having the first job. The employer is usually required to complete an official form for the permit application, on which he can state the length of the employment. If this is not done, the contract is considered of an indefinite duration and the residence permit should be for a long period. If the permit runs out before the job, then it can be renewed without difficulty. Officially, all EC countries issue five-year residence permits to working EC foreigners, but they often prefer to allow a shorter time initially, which can then be extended — if you are still working.

Though there are no longer visa restrictions, permit systems fulfil a similar function. Because, in theory, EC membership prevents barriers against the free movement of workers, many countries use the residence permit system to unofficially keep tabs on the numbers and quality of foreign workers. They discourage the jobless without admitting that they are really issuing visas and old-fashioned work permits. A rose by any other name . . .

YOUR EC RIGHTS

Yes, as a citizen of Europe you have rights; rights inscribed in black and white on the tablets of Community law. You may not realize it, possibly because you have not had to fight for those rights. Nonetheless, they are part of your birthright, and you should be ready to assert them.

As *Europeans, you have rights* states, all EC countries are supposed to treat each others' citizens in exactly the same way as their own in all areas of life and work. Thus, under EC regulations, if you already have a job you, your husband or wife and children are absolutely entitled to get a residence permit. You are all under the same social insurance and health care system as the citizens of the country in which you are employed. There should be no discrimination or distinction of an official, economic or social nature in your treatment by fellow EC members.

Having worked, you are then entitled to unemployment benefits under the system of the country in which you have become unemployed, if you qualify. Previous social insurance contributions paid in other countries may also be taken into account. Of course, different countries have varying ways of calculating entitlement and some have more generous allowances than others. For some, it takes a surprisingly short work period to qualify for benefits, especially if you have already paid contributions elsewhere. For example, in the Netherlands you must have paid social insurance contributions for 130 days in the previous 12 months, whereas in Germany you need only have worked and paid contributions for 26 weeks in the previous 3 years. Unfortunately, the countries with high social welfare payments are also the ones with high living costs (Denmark, for example). It is safe to say that no European country provides a life of luxury on the dole, no matter how astronomical the figures sound to our deprived ears.

Discrimination: Once you are working, there can be no discrimination against you in terms of salary or working conditions on the grounds of your nationality. You are also supposed to be treated in the same way as nationals of the country by official agencies, such as the youth information organisations, welfare agencies and national employment services. You are entitled to use their facilities and apply for jobs available through their offices. Employment offices only have the right to refuse to refer someone for a job if they consider his or her language is insufficient for the work involved.

Of course, the exalted ideals of the European Commission are a long way from the reality at ground level. The local official is faced with an outsider who is in direct competition with local people for the jobs available, an 'alien' who possibly cannot even speak the language properly. No EC directive can force people to be helpful or even polite and friendly. It is a common trait of all species to look after their own and the reaction to a German or an Italian looking for work in your local FAS office might not exactly be welcoming.

Protected areas: The only work areas which EC countries can officially protect are in public administration and the security forces. Basically, under Article 48 of the Treaty of Rome, governments have the right to exclude non-nationals from any post which they define as 'connected with the exercise of official authority'. This is broadly applied to the whole of the civil service in most countries.

Some professions protect themselves by refusing to recognise each others' qualifications and therefore the right to practise. This is frowned upon by the European Commission, who are currently working towards mutual acceptance of most professional qualifications by 1991 (*see also p. 65*).

HEALTH CARE AND THE E111

All EC members can have free or subsidised emergency health care when staying in another Community country, so long as they follow the regulations of the public health system of the country being visited. This is done through the E111 form (the certificate of entitlement to benefits in kind in the case of sickness or maternity) which is used throughout the EC.

The E111 is no longer restricted to those who have paid social insurance contributions. You do not have to have a PRSI (pay-related social insurance) number to be issued the form and there is no official limit to the period of cover you can request to be put on the form. It is not, however, a permanent arrangement and is intended to be used only in 'cases of immediate need of workers who are staying temporarily in a member state other than that in which they habitually reside'. In other words, the E111 is intended only for emergency care and not because other countries appear more attractive to be sick in.

When you apply for the E111, the duration of cover will depend on how long you say you intend to stay. Usually it is less than 3 months, but people who travel frequently or intend to stay for a long time may be issued the E111 for a period of up to one year. But it is no longer valid once you start a paid job (which, of course, is meant to happen within 3 months) and pay social insurance contributions. Once you are working, the national health service of the country involved is at your disposal, under the terms of entitlement and regulations of that country's system.

Intending students of a course of study in another member state are also provided for and would have better cover under the E109.

It is worth noting that despite the fact that the E111 is intended only for cases of immediate need, you should in many countries go first to their equivalent of the local health board with your E111 to find out how the system works, register if necessary and get a list of the doctors you can use. The local clinic or health board equivalent will tell you about the system and who pays what. It is better to know beforehand than to end up arguing feebly in a foreign language with the wrong kind of doctor who is demanding immediate payment of a huge bill.

There is no uniformity in the way EC countries administer health care on the basis of the E111. In some (eg Germany and Italy), a medical certificate proving entitlement is issued by the local health insurance office on production of the form (or, in Denmark, for example, when you join the national identity register); in others (such as the Netherlands), the E111 alone is your proof of cover for doctors, chemists and hospitals.

Though most general practitioners are part of the public health service in most countries, some are not and if you go privately you have to pay (usually the initial total cost) and then apply for a refund. In this case, the difference between the standard public health payment and your doctor's fee is your responsibility. You could also make the mistake of attending a doctor who does not accept public patients, in which case you must pay the entire fee.

Countries also vary in the way payment is organised. In some (eg France), you pay for treatment and prescriptions first and then get a rebate. Others (eg Denmark and the Netherlands) provide care without charge if you have the right form. Still others (eg Spain) are likely to argue that you can apply for a rebate in your own country, though they should not be able to do this if you have a long-term address and have found out about the local system.

Many countries' health services do not cover the total cost of care. A percentage or standard token payment is required from the recipient. In Germany, for example, a standard fee of DM2 is charged for each prescription, though the doctor's visit is free.

The hiccups in this common EC health care system are still being ironed out and people have had problems with acceptance of the E111 without prior registration and clearance from a clinic. Do not be put off by the term 'emergency care'. It has more to do with discouraging people from trying to get their long-standing complaints seen to because the queues are shorter in another country, than providing cover in a situation when you are almost too ill to do more than produce the form while being rushed off in an ambulance. It refers to the type of conditions for which you are covered rather than the way in which the form is to be used. Refunds are available if you end up having to pay for treatment when this shouldn't be the case, but getting money back is a slow, painful process.

The E111 form is available at your local Health Board office in Ireland and it has to be completed there. You should apply for it at least one month before you intend to leave. The Department of Health's very helpful European Information Unit can provide more data (*address on p. 112*) and they have also prepared a useful series of leaflets on the health care systems of various European countries.

TAXATION IN THE EC

Strangely, income tax is not yet subject to EC rules and has not been standardised in the Community. Our own dog's dinner of a tax system shows how complex this area is and how difficult it is to devise an equitable policy, even if the will is there. Nearly all EC countries operate a PAYE (pay-as-you-earn) system (*see p. 37*). Further information sources and more detail can be found under each EC country's entry.

Tax rates and bands vary widely between EC countries. As a very rough guide, the average worker on an average salary with average allowances can expect to lose about 30% of his or her income in tax.

Rules and requirements for personal taxation also vary from country to country and EC members are always subject to the legislation of the country in which they are working. While previous social insurance entitlements are transferred to the EC country in which you are working—and made equivalent in terms of that country's system (which, of course, may not be equal in quality or value) — income tax entitlements are, unfortunately, not transferred. The fact that most EC countries operate a PAYE system means that the deductions are made before you even see the money, usually on the basis of projections of your total income over the whole year which, possibly wrongly, assume that you will continue to earn at the same rate.

Therefore, if you take a job in another country and stay for the full tax year, you will probably be entitled to the normal allowances and reliefs of a resident. You could end up losing the average 30% of your pay in tax. If you do not stay for the full year, the deductions will have been made anyway on the basis of your projected income and so you may be entitled to a rebate of the excess tax already paid on the amount you actually earned or the portion of your total income which was considered taxable may be reduced.

Alternatively, the whole of your income may be considered liable for tax in accordance with residency requirements. These requirements vary, but often a working period of over six months is necessary before you are entitled to tax-free allowances. France, for example, imposes tax deductions retrospectively, so if you had no income in France in the previous tax year you will not be liable. Of course, if you stay into the following tax year you will be taxed on your income of the previous year.

Tax certificate: Most employers tend to put new employees on emergency tax until the position is clarified by the central tax authority. This means it is important to get a card, fiscal number or whatever is the local equivalent of the tax certificate from the local tax office as soon as possible when you begin work. Enlightened countries provide employers with forms for their staff to complete, which are then sent to the tax office who send back a certificate, thereby saving time and frustration. Who of us, having queued at an empty hatch in the bowels of some joyless tax office for hours and still not got the right form, would cry at this development in our own country?

Tax rebates: Any period of work in an EC country should be officially recorded for tax purposes. When you are leaving a job for any reason (and at the end of each tax year), your employer should produce some form of employee cessation certificate (the equivalent of the P45 and P60 in Ireland). This will record total pay, tax paid, total insurance contributions and the length of time for which you worked. Do not leave a job without this. If you have worked in a number of jobs, keep all the certificates. It is also useful to keep your payslips in case of any confusion. If you did not get a certificate for any reason (for example, from a very short-term job that you did not stick with long enough to complete the formalities), your payslip will be very important.

With this cessation-of-employment certificate, you can apply for a rebate from the local tax office. This normally happens at the end of the tax year, when you complete a tax declaration or return, and excess payment will be refunded.

If you are leaving the country before the end of the year, you must complete an application for a rebate before you leave. This will require you to state your date of departure and declare that you will not be working in that country again during that tax year. You will probably have to prove this by handing over your residence permit or showing your travel ticket. Otherwise, you could easily work elsewhere and get two lots of allowances. You will also have to give a forwarding address to which the rebate can be sent. It will probably take a long time to arrive. Applications for rebates are often not permitted until the end of the tax year or even, in the case of Denmark, are not issued until six months after the end of the year in which the tax was paid.

Student taxation: Students working in another EC country for a summer vacation can sometimes be exempted from tax, or get a refund the following year, if they can prove their student status and get the exemption beforehand. This is the practice in Germany and is worth investigating in other countries. There is usually a limit on either your monthly or gross income over which you will be liable for tax. There is also usually a limit on the length of time for which you can work to qualify for an exemption.

Students pursuing a course of study in another EC country are often issued residence permits on the understanding that they are permitted to work only part-time, for a certain number of hours per week. Some countries allow other EC full-time students, like their own, a certain income tax-free to be earned on a casual basis. More information on the work and tax position for students in other EC countries can be found in the *Student Handbook* (see p. 66).

SOCIAL SECURITY IN THE EC

Unemployment benefit, based on social insurance contributions (PRSI), is transferable between EC countries. You can claim it in another EC country, but only for 78 days and only provided you had qualified for, and had been registered (signing on) to draw unemployment benefit for at least 4 weeks in the country in which you last worked. Of course, you must possess the necessary forms and comply with the often complicated bureaucracy of the country involved. It is also necessary to sign on again within 7 days in the new country. More detail is given below.

Unemployment assistance (the dole) is not, however, transferable. Its existence and payment are seen as the responsibility of your own country. It is paid on the basis that you cannot support yourself, through an inability to get work, which is no fault of your own but rather of your country's economic problems. You are, theoretically, trying to find work. Each country also feels it is not their fault that you cannot manage to get work — they all have their own unemployment problems. Society still does not like to see people starving, but in the EC's mind, charity begins at home. In other words, if you are going to be unemployed, be unemployed in your own country.

The residence permit regulations (*see p. 44*) effectively prevent any alternative. As the *Guide for Young Visitors to Denmark* says, 'Even though they are in possession of a valid work-and-residence permit, EC citizens cannot expect to be unconditionally entitled to public assistance. . . The authorities always reserve the right to consider whether it is "convenient" that you stay in the country in the long run — or whether repatriation would be a better solution.'

That said, it is possible in some EC countries to be given discretionary assistance, if you are genuinely destitute, or have been working but do not yet qualify for unemployment benefit.

Transferring benefit/Form E303: In order to transfer your unemployment benefit to another EC country, you must have been signing on for at least 4 weeks and you must notify your local employment exchange that you intend to leave. One week is the very minimum notice to give; 3 or 4 weeks is preferable. The more notice you give, the less likelihood of delays at the other end. You may also need to give a forwarding address in the country in question.

Form E303 is produced by your local employment exchange and processed by the EIU (European Information Unit) of the Department of Social Welfare (*see p. 112*). This form states the number of days' assistance and the amount you are entitled to. This, in turn, is either handed to you to present to the local office where you are going (which will save you a lot of time) or it is sent to the relevant central social welfare office, where it is processed and translated before being sent on to the local office where you will make your claim.

Your unemployment benefit will be the same amount as you get in Ireland and will be paid for a maximum of 78 days in the new country. The rate of exchange of the amount you get here into local currency is agreed officially and adjusted from time to time, so it may not correspond exactly with commercial exchange rates. If your benefit entitlement is running out, you will receive what is left for that period, rather than the full 78 days. You may experience some difficulty transferring benefit if you have much less than 78-days entitlement remaining to you.

It is important that you register at the nearest local version of our employment exchange at your destination within 7 days of last signing here. Then you should keep signing on in the same way as you do here. Obviously, you must fulfil the same requirements — be available for work, be actively seeking employment, etc. The ability to speak the relevant language is useful and sufficient funds to deal with delays are essential (it can take a minimum of 4 weeks for your benefit to come through). Other EC countries have different signing and payment requirements; you may find yourself signing on fortnightly, for example, or even receiving the payment in two or three lump sums rather than in weekly issues.

You can make use of this provision only once between any two periods of employment. In other words, it is impossible to transfer benefit, work for a while and then transfer benefit again — unless, of course, you re-qualify.

After starting work, you have to go through the whole process of qualifying for benefit again, according to the requirements of the particular country. This is important in relation to coming home. If you receive benefit in another country for the maximum period allowed and then return to Ireland, your benefit having run out in EC terms, you will probably have to work and pay insurance contributions again before being entitled to claim. On the other hand, if you return before the 78-day period is up, it is a simple case of transferring a continuing claim, which will be available for whatever benefit period is left out of your original Irish possible maximum of 390 days. So, if you were entitled to more than 78 days on the basis of your contributions, you will not be able to get it unless you return, without having worked in the meantime, and sign on again here as soon as possible, within 7 days.

During the 78-day period, you can also transfer benefit to other EC countries, although you have to register again within 7 days in the new country.

Future claims: Everyone intending to work in Europe should get forms E104 and E301 before leaving Ireland. They are available from and prepared by the EC Records Office (*see p. 112*). They state your sickness and unemployment insurance benefit contributions here. Everyone (not only those transferring benefit) will find it more useful to have them in possession, already prepared in case the need arises. In relation to future unemployment or inability to work through illness in another country, these two forms provide the documentation you need in order to apply for social welfare.

Form E301 is especially useful to have with you. It details your insurance contributions during previous periods of work in Ireland and can be combined with your social insurance payments in the country in which you have most recently become unemployed. The combination may increase your entitlement or indeed qualify you for social security if you have not been working there for very long. Countries differ in the number of hours, days or months you need to have worked in order to qualify.

If you are a dependent family member of an unemployed person who qualifies for social security somewhere in Europe, as in Ireland, you could be covered for sickness and maternity benefits elsewhere through the E106. It is really intended for wives and families of workers who have paid contributions but now live on social security in another country than that of the dependant who is applying for aid.

The Department of Social Welfare provides a booklet about this confusing subject, entitled *SW49: Social security in the EC* (*see p. 126*). There is also a series of EC leaflets for different countries entitled *Social security for migrant workers.*

EC REGULATIONS IN A NUTSHELL

Specific information on EC residence requirements, taxation and health care is given in the separate sections for each country. But in the meanwhile, here is a summary of EC regulations:

- VALID PASSPORT: You can stay for 3 months, 'no restrictions'. You must have 'adequate funds' and may have to register as an alien. This requires a contact address and possibly proof of adequate financial resouces. An ID card may then be issued.

- RESIDENCE PERMIT: You will usually need one if you stay for longer than 3 months. This requires proof of employment or a definite job offer (in the form of a letter stating terms and duration of employment signed by the employer, or sometimes an official form, or payslips). Or it may require proof that you are studying full-time in an educational institute. Some countries will simply accept a permanent address and adequate funds.

- EMERGENCY HEALTH CARE: You are covered by form E111, available from your local Health Board. You may need to register and get a medical services card before receiving treatment. Once working, you are covered (to different degrees) by the State system. You need to register or join an insurance fund as soon as you begin work.

- UNEMPLOYMENT BENEFIT: Benefit is transferable and may be drawn in another country for a maximum of 78 days, provided you were signing on in Ireland, or another EC country, for at least 4 weeks before. Social insurance contributions may also be transferred to help you qualify for unemployment benefit in future, having worked for a certain period and become unemployed in another country. Unemployment assistance (the dole) is not transferable, but discretionary payments may be available, usually means-tested.

- HEALTH AND BENEFIT FORMS: To sum up,
  - E111 = certificate entitling you to medical care (emergency sickness or maternity treatment).
  - E109 = certificate entitling students to medical care.
  - E303 = certificate to tranfer umemployment benefit to another EC country. It states number of days you are entitled to claim for and your rate of pay.
  - E301 = your record of PRSI contributions, to use in future claims for unemployment benefit in other EC countries.
  - E104 = your record of PRSI contributions, to use in future claims for sickness benefit in other EC countries.
  - E106 = certificate for dependants of an unemployed person in another EC country, allowing transfer of sickness or maternity benefits.

4
The EC from this end

EC CHECKLIST

- valid passport
- birth certificate
- E111 form from Health Board
- E301 and E104 certificates from Department of Social Welfare
- translations of qualifications and curriculum vitae
- basic language ability
- adequate funds
- useful addresses

THE SINGLE EUROPE ACT AND YOUR OPPORTUNITIES

More and more money and effort is going to be expended on language learning, work experience programmes and educational exchange by the EC in the next few years. They are seen as key areas for the run-up to 1992. It makes sense that expenditure in these areas will go further towards making happy little Europeans of us all than expensive butter mountains. They will certainly be more accessible and enjoyable for those who keep tabs on what is available and take part. The rule is to keep your ear to the ground — and apply. One could be forgiven for thinking that there is funding available for almost anything and that sponsored holidays in the Costa del Sol are next on the list.

Among the language schemes that will be coming on line in the near future are free or subsidised language training in the Irish workplace and facilities for travel and exchange between workers and students of EC countries. The Lingus Programme for secondary schools and third-level institutions begins a phased introduction in the 1989-90 academic year. It will provide student and teacher exchanges between schools in different countries, better language teacher training and in-service training opportunities.

A new EC social programme has been adopted and should be operational by 1992. Its aim is to improve labour mobility. To this end, likely introductions are Community-wide compilation by computer of job opportunities, easing of taxation on workers permanently or regularly in a Community country other than their own, extension of the EC residence (work) permit to 10 years and transferable unemployment assistance payments to give someone on the dole the financial means to move to another EC member state with better job prospects. Schemes for greater employee involvement in company management and better insurance cover for health and safety in the workplace are also probable.

There is, however, a darker side to these schemes. They are all designed to ease worker mobility in the face of local or regional job losses throughout the EC caused by the single European market. The European Commission itself has estimated that the initial impact of 'deregulation' (the removal of protectionist barriers to free trade and the creation of an 'open' Europe) may result in the initial loss of 225,000 jobs in certain sectors and regions. Given their tendency to underestimate and adjust later (remember joining the Community of Nine in 1973 and the subsequent inflation?), the effect on job opportunity here, already limited, is bound to make Europeans of us all, sooner rather than later. As far as Ireland is concerned, such schemes to improve labour mobility will doubtless facilitate people who *want* to go and work elsewhere. It looks as though more people will be forced to make that choice or to look for another destination as our economy is weakened and unemployment problems become greater at home.

Increased migration of skilled workers from the poorer countries to the richer, industrialised ones has been predicted. An article in the *Sunday Press* of 31 July 1988 summed up the issues thus: 'If we really believe in a fully integrated market, it means that we must be able and willing to emigrate (without whingeing) to wherever in the Community workers are scarce. As it stands, 1992 could lead to an over-centralisation of Europe's economy in parts of Germany, France and the south-east of England. With nationalism, it might be possible for small countries like Ireland to produce strong independent companies with their headquarters in Ireland. After 1992, this could be very difficult; instead we could get regionalism which means humiliating hand-outs to countries such as Ireland. All ambitious people, however, would tend to emigrate once they had their basic education and try to cut into the prosperity in an increasingly congested centre.'

All of these exchange programmes and free language classes are there to ease the transition. They sweeten the pill of forced emigration.

LANGUAGE

When considering Europe as a possible destination, remember that language is the biggest barrier — and plan ahead. The first difficulty for the individual, regardless of EC regulations, and the most obvious is the need to communicate in the correct language. We all know exceptions, but the general rule for getting a job — even the worst kind of work anywhere — is being able to understand and respond. If you do not know the language, all but the most menial jobs are impossible. Conversely, it is surprising how little knowledge is needed before a potential employer can be impressed. Obviously, the more language you have, the better and wider your options.

While official EC literature is printed in all the Community languages, there is no obligation on member states to print their forms and residence permits in anything other than their own national language(s). Even if you can negotiate your way around the local bureaucracy, there is little likelihood of finding work or even surviving in a country without the help of some intelligent, intelligible speech. (The one EC exception to this for the average Irish monoglot, Britain, is outside the scope of this book.)

Thus, your first move must be towards learning a language, or at least gaining some knowledge of it. A crash course to improve on school French, German or Italian is the best option. Fluency is not necessary — just a working knowledge of everyday words and phrases to use for the first weeks. Since the best way to learn a language is to use it, regard a short course before you leave as an investment to ensure survival while you improve in the country itself. Once your language has improved — as it will very quickly with total immersion — you can use it as a selling point for better work. Once you know one language, others will come more easily. The most important step is to know some before you leave. Self-study with a good textbook or local nightclasses are often more useful than expensive language school tuition. The Spanish, French (Alliance Française), German (Goethe Institute) and Italian cultural centres provide language classes among their cultural and social activities.

Currently, the EC is concentrating on improving people's knowledge of Community languages. So you could well find *free* language classes or subsidised trips are available to help with your studies. The Association of Teachers of Italian is already providing language classes for Leaving Certificate in the Italian Cultural Institute (3 terms of 10 weeks each cost £180 in 1988). Make enquiries at the cultural centres, the EC Information Office or the YEB. Secondary school and third-level students of this decade will have far better language teaching than ever before, thanks to EC attention and the Lingus Programme, but for the rest of us it is never too late.

EC INFORMATION

The EC spends a lot of money on keeping its members informed of agreements, regulations and statistics. Countless publications are available at the EC Information Office in Dublin (*see p. 113*). While many are glossy public relations leaflets with little hard information, the library contains some useful directories and policy documents, as well as the addresses of organisations related to education and work in member states.

Similarly, all public libraries and local Community and Youth Information Centres (CYICs) are good sources for getting to know what's on offer. The CYICs are especially useful for information on EC-funded and international schemes available from Ireland. Simply pick your country, and they will be able to produce a file about organised opportunities there. The Dublin CYIC is in Sackville Place (*see p. 113*). The Dublin Central Library in the ILAC Centre has the equivalent of *Golden Pages* business directories for all the EC countries and lots more in their Business Information Centre.

There is also a series of EC-sponsored guide books, currently available for six countries. Published in association with the European Youth Information and Counselling Exchange (ERICYA), more editions, including an Irish one, are in preparation. The guide series is called *Young Visitors to ... Belgium/ Denmark/Great Britain/France/Spain/The Netherlands* (individual titles vary, *see p. 126*). They should be available from the EC Information Office, the YEB or local CYICs; they can also be bought in USIT (*see p. 113*), at a cost of IR£2.00 with ISIC card, IR£2.50 without.

Rather obviously aimed at young people, these guides provide an introduction to travel, study, life and work in the particular country, with lots of addresses and background information which would be useful to anyone. Their quality varies, however, and it is difficult to cope with strange translation and the 'youthful' style in which they are written. A sample from the health section of the French guide (in fact called *Hello France*) reads: 'Health is something for old folks to think about! When you're 20 and full of pep, you have loads of other things on your mind besides nursing every little hurt and it seems like a waste of time to look into the kind of health insurance you've got. But you never know. You might get a savage attack of Asian flu that drops you in your tracks or have a stupid accident, the kind that only happens to other people. Or maybe one of those sexually transmitted germs will find its way into your jeans. . . Yes, even the 15 to 25 crowd can run into health problems.' It then gives useful information and addresses for all aspects of health help in France.

EC OPPORTUNITES AVAILABLE FROM IRELAND

Exchange and training schemes: There are many agencies and organisations in Ireland offering all sorts of exchange and training schemes in other EC countries. All aim at making it easier and cheaper for the individual to get to Europe, for a long or a short time. The objectives of the schemes are varied and excellent opportunities are there for the taking, including:

- language learning
- cultural exchange leading to greater international understanding
- links of a lasting nature between schools, companies or cities
- vocational experience and training
- provision of trained workers to fill local shortages

If you look hard enough, there is bound to be something on offer that would further your aims. The only difficulty may be finding out about it. It is worth remembering that a lot of these schemes are EC-funded for your benefit and that local agencies are there to administer them on your behalf, not to dole them out like smarties they paid for with their own money.

In many ways you are lucky that you are thinking of going to Europe. It is rapidly becoming the most accessible and cheapest destination for Irish people, if they are prepared to go there under the auspices of official schemes. In the run-up to 1992, more and more movement of young people between countries will be organised. A tiny sample of what is on offer is mentioned below. Find out more from the information sources or agencies involved (*addresses listed on pp. 112-14*).

The Youth Exchange Bureau (YEB) was set up specifically to coordinate Ireland's participation in both EC-funded and international youth exchange schemes. It offers countless educational trips and vocational experience opportunities. Most schemes are part of the 'Youth for Europe' programme by which the EC intends, over a three-year period, to send 80,000 young people and 600 youth workers for at least a week (and often a lot longer) to another country in order to learn the language and experience culture and work there.

The YEB also operates the 'Wider Horizons' programme for the International Fund for Ireland, which provides travel to facilitate intercultural understanding between groups of young people from Northern Ireland and the Republic. They also operate some YWEP schemes (*below*). Regular bulletins are produced and provide a useful starting point for information on State-sponsored ways and means of getting to Europe.

FAS, Ireland's training and employment authority, administers a lot of interesting programmes. About half of its running costs come from the European Community, so it is to be expected that they will provide opportunities for would-be Irish 'young Europeans'. Among its schemes are the European Orientation Programme and the Young Worker Exchange Programme (YWEP).

The European Orientation Programme is organised by the Confederation of Irish Industry in collaboration with FAS. It sends graduates to EC countries to learn the language and gain work experience in a foreign business environment. The principal destinations are France and Germany, but more recently participants have been sent to Italy, Spain and Portugal. The scheme has been running since 1983 and more than 200 graduates have participated to date.

The Young Worker Exchange Programme (YWEP) sent about 400 people to Europe in 1988. There are short- and long-term programmes (some as long as 16 months), which consist of a period of language training followed by work experience. Basically, to be eligible for a YWEP you must be a national of an EC member state, 18-28 years old, have vocational training or practical work experience, have worked for a year and started work before the age of 20. In other words, it is aimed at those with practical and technical skills. You get excellent experience with good conditions: travel costs within the country and accommodation are paid for, pocket money (around IR£27.50 a week) and 75% of the cost of your return airfare. All the participant has to produce is 25% of the airfare and in some cases a satisfactory knowledge of French or German.

Generally, FAS deals with the skilled or professionally trained on YWEP and other schemes, while the YEB (*above*) is intended for students, youth groups, youth leaders and young people in general.

AFS — Interculture Ireland also runs work experience and exchange programmes, with European countries among its many destinations. The objective of AFS, a worldwide organisation, is to promote understanding and friendship between people of different nationalities and races. To this end, AFS has developed a Young Worker exchange programme (in collaboration with EFIL/European Federation for Intercultural Learning), giving young people the opportunity to discover new lifestyles and working methods. Available mostly in Community countries, the Young Worker exchange programme usually lasts for 3 weeks or 8 months (the latter includes a language course of 2 months followed by 6 months of paid work experience). AFS also runs a student exchange programme which lasts for one year.

IAESTE and AIESEC are two other organisations with opportunities for student exchange in EC countries (*see p. 31*).

There are numerous other groups — cultural, Christian, environmental; you name the interest, there is a scheme to get you there. Failing sources here, the British State organisation, CBEVE (Central Bureau for Educational Visits and Exchanges, *see p. 113*) publish books packed with information on this area, such as *Working Holidays 1989* (job opportunities in over 100 countries worldwide), *Volunteer Work* (information and addresses on over 100 organisations recruiting volunteers for projects in 153 countries worldwide) and *Help?! Guidelines on International Youth Exchange*. These books are available from Irish libraries, too.

FINDING WORK IN THE EC

Ireland's Department of Labour runs a service, called SEDOC, for people who wish to work in other EC countries (*see p. 112*). Aspiring workers can register by completing a form detailing education, language and work experience, and the country or countries in which employment is desired. This information will be kept on file and when SEDOC is notified of vacancies by other State employment agencies or private employers in the EC they pass on the details and addresses to suitable persons on their register. Since most embassies of EC countries in Ireland and many FAS offices refer almost any young person enquiring about work, either at home or abroad, to this organisation, SEDOC has many more people on file than job possibilities. However, it is worth registering with them anyway. People with trade qualifications or specific technical skills who have a clear destination in mind, fluency in the language in question and who want long-term work are most likely to have some joy of SEDOC.

A Community-wide, computerised clearing house of job vacancies is likely to come on stream in the near future. As the number of jobs actually available in these recessive times is unlikely to increase, the net effect within each EC country may be a natural inclination to fill the vacancy quietly from within, saving the massive application processing and intense competition which would be a result of greater publicity. Don't forget that Ireland's unemployment problem is not unique when thinking about work in Europe. Our unemployment rate is, however, about 8% higher than that of most other EC countries.

Work in the European Commission, 'stages' and schools: You can work in the EC Commission in a variety of capacities. Usually, you need to be a graduate of a third-level institution with a degree or diploma equivalent, under 30 and speak another Community language as well as your mother tongue. Information can be obtained from the Department of Foreign Affairs (*see p. 112*).

Jobs in the European Commission are also advertised from time to time in the national newspapers. For all of them, you need to be high-powered in the particular field required (secretarial, clerical or whatever) and also proficient in at least two languages other than your own. Competition is intense.

Among the best-known schemes for aspiring workers in Europe is the traineeship, or 'stage'. You can be a 'stagiare' for one year, sometimes extended for another six months. These schemes are intended to provide periods of experience after vocational training (*see also p. 31*).

Language assistantships have been popular among teachers and recent graduates for many years. To be an 'assistant' in a school in another country (from here, usually France, Spain or Germany), you need to be a graduate or prospective graduate under 30 who intends to teach the language involved. You teach 12 hours a week, get low but just adequate pay, and receive medical insurance. Application forms and information are usually available in April, for application by early May for the following school year, from Office 2 of the Department of Education (*see p. 112*). The YEB also runs assistant schemes (in Canada) for French teachers.

EDUCATION WITHIN THE EC

Academic recognition of qualifications: There is an EC policy to standardise and recognise all degree or diploma courses at Community level. This is especially important for professionals who may find themselves effectively barred from practice in another member state. An element of self-interest and protectionism is behind a reluctance to recognise other countries' professional qualifications. So far, doctors, nurses, veterinary surgeons, dentists, midwives, architects and pharmacists, among others, are entitled to register as professionals and to work throughout the Community. But there are other fields, notably engineering, where this is not yet the case.

This situation will have to change by 1992, to ensure the envisaged free movement of workers within the EC. To this end, a general directive on the recognition of professional qualifications was adopted in July 1988 covering a wide range of professions. Basically, it will affect the majority of people who hold a degree, diploma or certificate of more than 3 years' education and training at higher level, which is recognised as adequate for the pursuit of a regulated profession in their own country. There is a slight possibility that such people will have to take a test or spend a period in practice under the supervision and training of a qualified member of the profession in the EC country concerned.

The professions involved are diverse: chartered surveyors, foresters, librarians, gas engineers, town planners and physiotherapists, to mention a few. A formal application for recognition has to be made, with all the documents, to the competent body in the host member state, who can take a maximum of four months to examine the application. Unfortunately, it takes a lot longer than this to introduce such wide-ranging regulations and it will be a minimum of two years before the graduate with professional training can be sure of official acceptance everywhere. Of course, no EC directive can force one professional to welcome another into his cosy establishment just because his qualifications are officially valid.

A network of National Academic Recognition Information Centres, affectionately known as NARCs, has been set up throughout Europe to liaise with educational institutions and to deal with academic recognition of qualifications. The Careers

Advisory Service in your third-level institution, your relevant professional organisation or, failing these, the helpful people in Dublin's NARC (*see p. 112*) will tell you about the standing of your own academic qualification within the EC, both for work and educational purposes.

Students: For those thinking of furthering their education, the *Student Handbook: Higher Education in the European Community*, published under the auspices of the EC Commission, gives a guide to courses and institutions in all member countries, as well as some useful background information on residence permits, the cost of living and student life. You can peruse it in the EC Information Office library, among other places, or order it from a bookshop. (Kogan Page are the British publishers.)

Transfer schemes: If you are engaged in full-time university study in Ireland, there are schemes to encourage movement between universities. Look for the ERASMUS (European Community Action Scheme for the Mobility of University Students) programme. Its aim is to promote broad and intensive cooperation between university-level institutions in all EC member states, through increasing the number of students who spend at least part of their university course in an institution in another member state, encouraging exchanges of university staff and developing a pool of graduates with direct experience of intra-Community cooperation. It provides financial support for students carrying out a period of study in other member states. Under this scheme, periods of study abroad are recognised as an integral part of the student's course in the home university and would be credited as part of the final degree or diploma.

COMETT (Community Action Programme for Education and Training for Technology) aims to foster greater cooperation between universities and industry. Among its activities is a European network for university-industry training partnerships. Graduates and academic staff may exchange with firms and institutions in other member states.

There is an EC-sponsored scholarship available for almost every area of study. For example, law students can compete for a year spent in Brussels, studying the legal institutions of the EC. Your faculty or the Department of Education will know what is available in your area.

5
The EC:
Country by Country

BELGIUM

BACKGROUND INFORMATION

Belgium is a small country. Its total area, of approximately 30,500 square kilometres, contains almost 10 million inhabitants, so the population density is high, with 323 people per square kilometre. It is also highly urbanised, with only 7% of the population living outside the cities.

Brussels (population almost 1 million) is the capital and the headquarters of the European Commission. Other important cities are Antwerp (500,000), Liège (500,000), Ghent (250,000) and Bruges (119,000). Politically, there is a constitutional monarchy and the government tends to be right of centre. The currency is the Belgian franc (Bfr56 = IR£1 — financial rate). Roman Catholicism is the majority religion. There are three major languages spoken — French and Dutch/Flemish (the official national languages), and German. The majority, in the Flanders region in the northern half of the country, speak Dutch or Flemish. French is the main language of Brussels and the southern part. The German-language region, in the east, is very small, with 0.67% of the population.

Belgium is bordered by France, Luxembourg, Federal Republic of Germany and the Netherlands, and has only 66 kilometres of coastline, on the North Sea. It has three major sea-ports, including Antwerp, and strong economic links with Luxembourg. It also has a possibly undeserved reputation for being the most boring country in Europe.

VISAS AND PERMITS

Irish citizens do not need a visa or work permit in order to work in Belgium. They do, however, require a residence permit in order to work legally, which amounts to the same thing. For the first three months, if you are staying in tourist-type accommodation and not working you do not have to do anything about identity registration. If you are not in tourist accommodation, you have to register.

Belgium seems to be one of the more complicated EC countries in which to live and work legally. A residence permit will be 'delivered by the communal authorities upon presentation of an Irish passport and evidence of employment'. This is all the information the Belgian Embassy in Dublin is prepared to give the casual enquirer. It seems that the system is to register at the local Town Hall within eight working days of arrival and the authorities (administration communale) will then issue a certificate (attestation d'immatriculation, modèle B). This will be valid for the 'length of your business' in Belgium.

If you are not working, it seems more likely that you will get a declaration of entry, or provisional registration certificate, valid for three months. This is a type of identity card and the authorities are keen that everyone should have one. If you get a job, you will get a full residence permit, valid for one year.

WORK

Belgium has never been a popular destination for the casual job-seeker. With the exception of EC-generated employment in either the high-powered clerical/secretarial field, in an institution of the EC or an agency serving it (for which a high standard of skill and several languages are needed) or in the hotel and catering area, few jobs are available in this highly industrialised country. Main industries are metallurgy (principally steel and iron), mechanical engineering and chemicals.

Belgium has a high unemployment rate by EC standards — 12.3% in 1986. The national employment office is ONEM (Office National de l'Emploi) and there are also private agencies. Advertisements may be found in *The Bulletin*, an English-language weekly published in Belgium.

TAXATION

Income tax is levied at a progressive rate on all annual incomes, in a PAYE system with similar bands and allowances to that in Ireland. Tax concessions are available for foreign workers who are not permanently resident in Belgium. Professional advice within the country is recommended.

Three deductions are made from every pay packet — social security (to the ONSS/Office Nationale Securité Sociale), health insurance (to a 'mutualité') and income tax (précompte professionnel).

HEALTH

The E111 covers you for emergency treatment. Once working, all employees pay into an insurance fund (mutualité). You have to pay for a doctor's visit and for prescriptions, but up to 80% of the cost is reimbursed. It may take six months of contributions to a fund to be fully covered, although PRSI contributions paid in Ireland are, of course, transferable (*see p. 54*).

DENMARK (DK)

BACKGROUND INFORMATION

Denmark is slightly larger than Switzerland, about 44,000 square kilometres. It consists of the peninsula of Jutland, which borders the Federal Republic of Germany, and about 400 islands. Norway and Sweden are close neighbours. There is unrestricted movement for living and working among the Scandinavian countries and their languages are mutually intelligible (*see also p. 97*). The population of over 5 million is highly urbanised, with 1.4 million living in the metropolitan area of Copenhagen, the capital city.

Many Danes speak fluent English, but as it says in the Embassy's rather general but useful hand-out *Working in Denmark*, 'Your attention is drawn to the fact that many jobs will require that you speak and write Danish.'

Denmark has among the highest per capita income and standard of living in the EC. Taxes and the cost of living are also very high, with food and accommodation using up much of the average wage, which was 90 Danish krone per hour in 1987 (Dkr10 = IR£1). The unemployment rate is now around 10%, but Irish people do find work and the country is rewarding to visit, with friendly people, great scenery and a liberal, though hard-working lifestyle, as well as being the only EC member (and therefore the most accessible) of the Scandinavian countries.

Ireland and Denmark have strong commercial links and it may be possible to establish useful contacts or find out about jobs on offer from this end. The Irish-Danish Business Association was established in 1987 and hopes to 'develop and stimulate the industrial, commercial and cultural relationship between Ireland and Denmark with participation of the young generation'. The Association cooperates with AIESEC (Ireland) on youth exchange programmes for students of business and management. Principally involved with commercial contacts for export businesses, the organisation has produced a useful magazine, *Ireland-Denmark: A Business Guide*, which contains a directory of businesses in Ireland with Danish links.

VISAS AND PERMITS

The Irish citizen with a valid passport may stay for a period of three months in Denmark without a visa or residence permit. Customs officials at point of entry may enquire into your financial circumstances and will expect you to have either a return ticket or enough money in hand to get home again.

According to the Danish Embassy in Dublin, you are expected to notify the local office of the National Register (Folkeregisteret) within five days of your arrival in the country if you intend to stay for more than three months and are on more than a tourist visit. When you register, they issue a certificate (personnummerbevis) containing your personal registration, or identity, number (personnummer). This is essential for all dealings with the authorities and opening a bank account. The number given includes your birthdate and is used as the main identification mechanism in all public files. It should be taken care of, since it is open to misuse.

However, you are generally expected to be working in order to get a personal registration number, since you have to produce a residence permit — for which you need a job! So, there is little chance of getting the personnummer until you have found work. Requirements for the personnummer are a residence permit and a permanent address. Any change of address must be notified within five days.

As well as a personal registration number, you will be issued with a social security certificate (sygesikringsbevis). This allows access to the national health service and free medical treatment.

A residence permit should be applied for as soon as you begin work or no later than two weeks before the end of the initial three-month period. If you do not have work at the end of these three months, there is little chance of getting a residence permit. It is only issued if your job fulfils certain minimum requirements related to working hours, salary and duration of employment, and you will need written confirmation of these details from your employer. The permit is also only granted if you have joined an insurance, or unemployment, fund (A-kasse) and you will need to present documentary proof of this, too. In addition, you will need to produce your passport and some photographs. With all these papers in order, you can obtain the residence permit from the local police or aliens department (Direktoratet for Udlændinge, *see p. 117*).

WORK

People with technical skills (engineering, plumbing, mechanics) are most likely to find good long-term work in Denmark. Sources to try are the equivalent trade union, job ads in newspapers or placing your own (*Berlingske Tidende* or *Jyllands Posten* are the main Danish papers, *see p. 117*). There are also local labour exchanges or you can write directly to the State Employment Service office in Copenhagen (Arbejdsformidlingen).

Private employment agencies (vikarbureaux) are good sources to try when in Denmark. Nurses could contact the Danish State Hospital directly or the Danish Association of Nurses (*see p. 117*). Casual work is available mostly in fast-food restaurants, hotels and factories. Agricultural work is surprisingly difficult to find, although seasonal workers are employed between June to October. Exchange programmes and workcamps are a popular means of visiting this expensive country.

TAXATION

Denmark has the highest rate of direct taxation in the EC. It is a PAYE system on a percentage basis, which works out at about 50% of the average salary. Deductions are made by the employer on the basis of your tax certificate (skattekort), provided by the local authority in the town hall (Rådhus). There is supposed to be a special allowance for foreign workers and no tax liability in certain cases for stays of less than 183 days by nationals of countries which have a double-taxation agreement with Denmark. But you need to be sure of your position and be prepared to fight for lower tax rates. Again, specialist advice is recommended. The accountants Coopers and Lybrand in Copenhagen produce a booklet *Expatriates in Denmark*, with information on common tax issues (see p. 117).

Everyone must also contribute to an insurance fund (A-kasse or arbejdsløshedskasser) for unemployment benefits. To become a member of these funds, which are usually associated with the relevant trade union, you must prove that you have had, or will have, five weeks of work. In order to get benefit, you must usually have been a member of such an insurance fund for a year and worked for six months during that period. Of course, contributions paid in other EC countries can be taken into account (see p. 54).

Everyone gets 12.5% of their total wages in holiday pay (feriepenge), which can be obtained through a Feriegirokort issued by the Feriegiro office and cashable at any post office. Unfortunately, you do not get it until the following year's holidays!

HEALTH

With the E111 form in your possession, the local branch of the social and health authority (Social-og Sundhedsforvaltning) can give you a list of doctors and dentists in the public health service to whose free services you are entitled. Prescribed medicine is paid for in part by the health service at one of two rates: 75% or 50% depending on the category of the drug. Hospital care is also free of charge. In an emergency, bring your E111 to the hospital; otherwise, the local health department will advise you.

Once working, or once you have a social security certificate/ health services card (sygesikringsbevis), you are covered by the same system as Danish workers. This card entitles you to free medical treatment by a local general practitioner of your choice, hospital care and some other services.

FRANCE

BACKGROUND INFORMATION

France has a population of 55.2 million and a population density of 101 per square kilometre. The language is French and very little else is spoken by a people notorious for their linguistic chauvinism. The capital, Paris (population 9 million), is the centre of government and administration, although France has several sizeable regional centres, including Marseilles and Lyons (both with populations of approximately 1.2 million), Grenoble, Bordeaux, Lille, Toulouse and Strasbourg. Inflation has come down to a 1988 level of around 3.5% (FRf9 = IR£1).

Unemployment is high, at over 10%. But the work that is available, the lower cost of living and the existence of a widely accepted national minimum wage (le SMIC, which was FRf27.57 per hour on 1 March 1987) all make France an encouraging destination for many Irish people. It is especially popular with students, for the easy pickings in seasonal tourist or agricultural work, and with lovers of the lifestyle and the renowned Gallic charm. Some French is a necessity. Otherwise, it is one of the easier European countries in which to survive, aided by the fact that there are lots of employment and information agencies to help you on the way.

VISAS AND PERMITS

In order to stay in France for up to 90 days, EC nationals need only a valid passport, whether they are working or not. After this period, you must apply for a residence permit (carte de séjour temporaire). There are four categories for this permit, which is usually valid for one year. You will be categorised as either a visitor, student, family member or wage-earner, requiring different documentary proof in each case. The work category is usually only granted if you can produce proof from your employer in the form of a signed confirmation of employment (déclaration d'engagement). If your term of employment is longer than a year (and this is stated on the employer's declaration), you can be given a 5-year temporary resident's card (carte de séjour de ressortissant d'un état de membre de la CEE).

You can get both the application forms for a carte de séjour and the official form the present or potential employer has to complete from the local police station (préfecture) or town hall (Mairie) in the place you intend to live. Or you can get them in Paris from the central police station (see p. 118). You need to produce your passport and sometimes a birth certificate, though this is not actually official policy. The French seem to set particular store by birth certificates and often want the original full version or a certified copy, sometimes even in translation. So bring it along, just in case.

People under 18 years of age must have parental consent to work in France and are forbidden certain types of work, such as in bars. The safety of foreign minors is a major preoccupation to the French; the police are likely to examine closely people who look young and even recommend that they go home for their own good if they appear vulnerable.

WORK

From this end: The French Embassy in Ireland produces a very useful booklet called, believe it or not, *Working in France.* This gives lots of information and addresses, and is especially good on employment sources for au pairs and those interested in agricultural work. The French Cultural Centre in Dublin, the Alliance Française, could be useful for other information and establishing contacts as well as language classes (see p. 118). The CBEVE also publish a jobs directory, *Work in France (see p. 63)*.

In France: The Agence Nationale pour l'Emploi (ANPE) is the State employment agency, but it deals with only 20% of the jobs market. There are also State and private agencies especially for young people looking for casual or temporary work, such as CIJs (centres information jeunesse) and the Ludéric chain (see p. 118).

The main newspapers carrying advertisements for work are *Le Figaro, France Soir* and *Libération,* the latter being particularly good for casual work. Jobs can be found in hotels and tourism centres, agricultural areas and as au pairs and group leaders (animateurs) for French summer camps. The long-term work that is available is as varied as there are occupations — but note, good French is essential. Secretaries and sales personnel, in particular, seem to find openings.

TAXATION

Personal income tax and social insurance contributions are lower in France than in many European countries, although the employer's contribution to social insurance is very high. The Irish worker whose salary is paid in France is liable to personal income tax (impôt sur le revenu) which is global, charged on all sources of income (not just salary) and at a series of rates. There is a system of allowances and exemptions, as in Ireland. The 'Conseiller fiscal' of the French Embassy in London may be able to provide more specific information (*see p. 118*).

HEALTH

With the E111, you are entitled to emergency treatment only. The local social insurance office or health clinic will have a list of doctors whose fees are reimbursable, after treatment. If you go to private practices, you have to pay the difference between the official rate, covered by social insurance, and the fee charged. The standard GP's fee is about FRf80 for a visit. You must pay the doctor or dentist's bill first and then get a fee sheet (feuille de soins) from him, which is an official form stating the treatment and fee charged. This must be brought to your local social insurance office, which will repay you from the sickness insurance fund (caisse primaire d'assurance maladie). Drugs and prescriptions can be refunded, in part or in full, if you include the prescription or label of the product with the fee sheet. Hospital treatment is also covered.

As soon as you take up employment, you should be part of the social security scheme and paying a percentage of your earnings, deducted by your employer, as a social insurance contribution. With the assistance of your employer, you should register with the local social security office (ONSS/Office Nationale Securité Sociale), which will issue you with a card and social security number. This entitles you to certain benefits, including fairly comprehensive health care, according to the number of contributions you have made, which is based on the number of hours you have worked.

GERMANY

BACKGROUND INFORMATION

The Federal Republic of Germany (simply called Germany here) is a large area of almost 249,000 square kilometres, with a great variety of people, dialects and landscape. It has a central position in Europe, bordered by 9 countries (Denmark, the German Democratic Republic, Czechoslovakia, Austria, Switzerland, France, Luxembourg, Belgium and the Netherlands). The population is 61.6 million, giving a density of 245 people per square kilometre. Principal cities are Bonn, the federal capital (population 300,000), Munich (1.3 million), Frankfurt (650,000), Cologne, Dusseldorf and the principal port of Hamburg (1.7 million). Some 10% of the population live in the industrial Ruhr area. West Berlin (almost 2 million) has a special position, isolated by GDR (German Democratic Republic) territory.

Germany's population has been decreasing since the middle of the last decade, despite the extensive use of foreign labour recruitment, especially of Turkish workers, until relatively recently. Germany still has a huge population of foreign workers and their families (4.3 million) and the institutions and organisations of the State are very much geared to helping the migrant worker with information and advice. An example of this is the excellent booklet available from the German Embassy in Dublin, entitled *Bundesverwaltungsamt (Federal Office of Administration): Information booklet for migrant workers and emigrants, No. 119*. Its 99 pages are packed with background information for the migrant. The large foreign population also makes survival easier for the non-German speaker.

Politically, Germany is a parliamentary democracy with a written constitution (Grundgesetz or Basic Law), which came into force in 1949. Bonn is the centre of government and the federal capital. The currency is the Deutschmark (DM2.66 = IR£1). The economy of this highly industrialised country is very strong and the rate of inflation minimal. Unemployment was around 9% in 1988. Despite this, West Germany has long been a major source of highly paid temporary employment for Irish students and of professional experience for science, computing and engineering graduates.

VISAS AND PERMITS

Irish and other EC nationals need only a valid passport. No work or residence permit is necessary for the first three months, but after this period a residence permit must be obtained and should be got as soon as you take up employment.

People intending to stay in the country for longer than one month, whether working or not, have to register with the local registration office (Einwohnermeldeamt) within one week of entry. Any change of address should also be notified within 7 days to the office for your area.

There is a special form for registration (Meldeschein), available at most stationery shops. It must be signed by the owner of your place of residence and by yourself. A certificate is issued confirming the registration. This formality is already fulfilled if you are staying in an hotel or hostel, by completion and signature of a special registration form. But it should not be overlooked if you are staying in private accommodation, since it could influence the outcome of your application for a residence permit. The registration certificate form is completely separate from the residence permit, but it may be required when you apply for the permit, so it is a formality worth observing.

The residence permit (Aufenthaltserlaubnis) is issued by the Foreign Nationals or Aliens Authority (Ausländerbehörde) in the town or district (Kreis) where you are living. Your local police station should be able to give you an application form (Anmeldungformula) and tell you where to go for a permit, usually the town hall (Rathaus). You will need some passport photographs and proof of employment (a signed job offer or payslips). If you don't have a job, proof of sufficient funds (eg a statement from a German bank account) and somewhere secure to live are required. You will also probably need to produce an endorsed registration form. In the case of intending students, a certificate of admission to the educational institution will be required. Anyone may also be requested to supply an official health certificate, which is a form that must be signed by a German doctor stating that you are in good general health. In practice, few escape this medical check.

WORK

There is ample work to be found in Germany, in both the casual areas of food-processing factories, hotels and building sites, and in the career area, especially for those with secretarial skills and languages, and for those with scientific or technical qualifications.

From this end: You can write directly to the central placement office of the Federal Employment Service (Zentralstelle für Arbeitsvermittlung) in Frankfurt (*see p. 118*), which deals with all overseas applications. If you have a particular trade or skill that is in demand, you may be lucky.

There is also a section in the central placement office for short-term summer employment for students. To be considered, you need written confirmation from your place of study in Ireland that you are registered as a full-time student. The work is mostly in hotels, restaurants and factories. You should apply before March for the following summer. The same office can also help with information for au pair work (*see also p. 116*).

Many people have found seasonal work in the smaller family-run hotels in Germany to be almost inhuman, demanding constant hard work and robotic efficiency. Some German food-processing factories recruit in colleges in Ireland, though the reputation of Irish students has been damaged over the years by incidents of rebelliousness at the conveyor belts in reaction to generally mind-bendingly boring work.

In Germany: The State-run Employment Offices (Arbeitsamter) are almost the only official agencies in Germany and it is possible to get work, especially casual or temporary jobs, through them. Private employment agencies are discouraged by the State. Possession of a curriculum vitae and references (Zeugnisse) in German, a contact phone number and the ability to speak German during your interview make it more likely that you will be given the same facilities as a German national, as is your due under EC regulations.

TAXATION

Anyone having ordinary or permanent residence for more than six months of the fiscal year in Germany is liable to income tax, which is imposed in an increasing scale on earnings above

DM4536 per annum. Like practically everywhere, there are various allowances for expenses and dependants but, unlike everywhere, there is a separate church tax of between 8 and 10%. Generally, you can expect to pay about 30% of your income to the taxman.

At the beginning of each calendar year, or when you begin work for the first time, you must get a tax card (Lohnsteuerkarte) from the local offices of the municipal administration (Rathaus). This details your tax category and tax-free allowance, and must be given to your employer, who will complete the gross earnings and deductions when you leave or when the end of the year comes. If you have several jobs you need several tax cards.

Student taxation: If you are a student who intends working for less than six months, you may apply for exemption before you get the tax card (*above*). It is most important to do this before the card is issued, since it states your tax category.

In order to qualify for exemption from income tax, health insurance, unemployment and pension scheme contributions, you need to apply in advance and fulfil the following conditions:

- a letter or some written confirmation from your Irish Institute of Higher Education, stating that you are a registered student;
- get employment related to your studies;
- work for no longer than 183 days;
- earn a gross income of no more than DM1000 per month.

If, however, you work for longer than six months, you must pay full contributions from the date you start work. You can then apply for a tax rebate the following year, but other deductions are not refundable. You should organise your own health cover, either through the E111 or a private scheme.

HEALTH

The local health insurance offices (AOK/Allgemeine Ortskrankenkassen) issue the German equivalent of a medical insurance certificate (Krankenschein) to those entitled on the basis of the E111. They will also provide information on practitioners you may attend. With the certificate you will be treated free of charge, although there is a fee of DM2 for each medicine prescribed, payable to the chemist. You may also have to pay the full cost if the drugs for your ailment are not serious enough. For example, 'In case of minor health disorders, as cough, cold, constipation, medicine will not be refunded', says the *Information booklet for migrant workers and emigrants, No. 119.*

Hospital treatment is directed by the doctor, who gives the patient a certificate to be presented to the local health insurance office. It, in turn, gives the intending patient a certificate of entitlement to treatment in a public ward (Kostenuberahmeschein), to be given to the hospital authorities. There is a nominal fee of DM5 per day in hospital, to be paid by any patient over 18, for a maximum of 14 days in any calendar year. If you are unlucky enough to need more time, it is free. In an emergency the hospital should accept the E111, but it is always better to have gone to the local health authority before the need arises.

Once you are working, social insurance contributions are deducted automatically from your wage. Your employer will register you and apply for an insurance number. You will be given an insurance identity card to use when registering with medical and unemployment authorities. You need a medical insurance certificate (Krankenschein) when treatment is required. This is valid for each current quarter and is available from the local authority or, in many cases, the employer. The employer may produce a booklet of them (Krankenscheinhefle) when you begin work, to be completed and signed each quarter as needed.

It is worth noting in relation to health care that many large German companies and factories have their own clinics and staff are encouraged to use them.

ITALY

BACKGROUND INFORMATION

Italy is, like Ireland, a major recipient of EC aid. It is, however, considerably more developed industrially and its population, of over 57 million, has a higher per capita income and lower cost of living than that of Ireland. It has never been a popular destination for Irish workers, largely because of the importance of speaking Italian for most work. The tendency, until recently, of the Irish education system to concentrate on French and German as the main continental languages has militated against it.

Italy differs from its northern neighbours in the degree to which it is multilingual, the slow process of 'Europeanisation' meantime creating demand for those proficient in more than one language. Its sunny climate, relaxed lifestyle and scenic and cultural assets should attract more people, especially since Italian classes are becoming increasingly popular as people realise the usefulness of the language on the jobs market and its easiness to learn.

Italy has miles of coastline and a major tourist industry, extending as it does into the Mediterranean from a position in the heart of Europe, bordering France, Switzerland, Austria and Yugoslavia. The monetary unit is the lira (IT*l* 1965 = IR£1). The major economic problem, inflation, is improving with membership of the EC and it is now running at about 5%. Unemployment is quite high, at about 13% (11.1% in 1986).

Rome (population 3.1 million) is the capital, centre of government and headquarters of many businesses. The north of the country is more industrialised, with Milan (1.6 million) as the major city of industry and commerce, followed by Turin (1.2 million) and Genoa. Government is by parliamentary democracy, usually by rather shaky coalitions, the main forces being the Christian Democrats and several Communist groupings.

VISAS AND PERMITS

As with all EC countries, a valid passport, but no visa, is needed by Irish citizens. A type of identity registration certificate (permesso di soggiorno) is required of those who wish to stay *longer than three days* and should definitely be got by those who intend to work.

This involves registering with the police authorities (questura) at the local station (*see p. 119*). They issue a permit valid for three months, which can then be renewed. Notification of arrival to the police usually happens automatically when you register in an hotel, pensione, hostel or campsite. But if you wish to stay for a period of time, it is important to get this 'permesso', which acts as a form of identity card while looking for work or having an extended holiday. Evidence of sufficient funds is not officially required but, as usual, a lot depends on the local police officer involved. Bring your passport and some photos to the office.

Once you are working, you need a work paper (libretto del lavoro). This is not officially a work permit, since none is needed under EC rules. You apply for it from the local Ispettorato del Lavoro and you need a contract or an official letter stating the terms of your employment from your employer. There should be no difficulties with this, although it can take longer than two weeks to come through. Your employer should help, since your possession of this work paper is required of him for tax and insurance purposes.

If you enjoy Italy and wish to stay, then you can apply for residency, which is available after a certain period of living and working in the country. But there is no need for a residence permit (permesso di residenza) once you begin work.

WORK

With Italian, many employment opportunities exist in the areas of tourism, public relations, business and financial management (throughout the country, but principally in Milan and Rome), and in commercial and secretarial companies in any business centre. The bilingual secretary, or anyone clerically skilled, with good Italian, is almost guaranteed work.

Casual work, of the bar or restaurant kind, is quite hard to organise from Ireland, although you could try writing to the larger hotels in major cities or resort areas, especially the ones with chains or related groups of hotels. The best approach is to do a thorough job-hunt on the spot in popular resort areas. The State employment service (Ufficio del Lavoro) is probably only useful as a last resort because of the high level of unemployment in Italy.

Without Italian, or while improving your spoken language, teaching of English as a foreign language is the best option. Many schools will be happy with a basic TEFL diploma and the extra money commanded by a degree and teaching qualification is not great. People with degrees could try for a job as a reader/lecturer in one of the many universities that take English speakers. Italy can be one of the more difficult EC countries in which to gain recognition of third-level qualifications. It is up to the individual employer or the relevant Italian authorities to recognise them as being equivalent to their own. The Italian Cultural Institute in Dublin (see p. 119) will translate and authenticate degrees and diplomas for you before you go.

From this end: Some Italian sales companies advertise in the Irish papers from time to time. The following are typical examples:

'Opportunities in Italy. Due to demand in the market we require extra Sales Personnel to travel and work throughout Italy. No knowledge of Italian required as on-the-job training is provided. Good renumeration for hard work and an opportunity to learn the language. Interviews held in Dublin, parents welcome at interview, only non-smokers need apply.'

(*Sunday Press*, 7 Aug. 1988)

'International Company, Cultural Contact . . . requires 4 persons, 18-23, bright and hard-working to sell language courses in Italy. Salary basis. No experience necessary as full training given. French speaking an advantage.'

(*Irish Independent*, 23 Sept. 1988)

Irish au pairs are popular in Italy. Irish and British agencies (see p. 115) always have work available and if you can overcome the fact that Italian children are usually over-indulged by our standards, it is quite a good country for this kind of work. Since au pair positions are classified by law as domestic employment, the family must pay the minimum wage according to the Collective National Contract for the number of hours worked each day and also pay contributions for medical and health insurance. A statement of terms and conditions is therefore needed from the prospective employer. In addition, the au pair must have an identity registration certificate (permesso di soggiorno).

As with most countries, horror stories of au pair jobs abound. This account appeared in the *Sunday Tribune* on 28 August 1988:

'...went to Milan to be au pair to a millionaire's family. He jumped naked through a window. She cried. Children cried. No English was spoken. But she lived to tell the tale ... I survived my eight weeks. It was a battle, and although unbruised I was always bursting with frustration. I could warn, or advise, other Irish teenagers of the advantages and disadvantages of the au pair circus on the continent, and especially in Italy. But au pairing is all about personal experiences.

'The experience was not forgettable. I earned IR£100 a week, both before and after my boss escaped through the window. It was a matter of survival, and I succeeded — against the odds and three Italian children. For most of the time I took charge of the children in a seaside resort outside Genoa called Alassio. But first the new au pair had to meet the family in Milan. The door was padlocked ... after some time, Mrs ... opened the door and said, "I have to go out for an hour, the children are down there." With that, she went!

'I wish I could say that I left triumphantly, or that the children stood crying their eyes out as they begged me to stay. I did leave though, with a good tan and a much greater appreciation of my home and Ireland — and au pairing. But I am returning next summer. To Italy and to Milan, and hopefully to a less eccentric family. '

TAXATION

Income tax in Italy is comparatively low, beginning at about 22%. Local municipal taxes are also deducted. Touche Ross International of Dublin produce a useful publication, entitled *Tax Investment Profile — Italy* (see p. 119).

HEALTH

Form E111 must be presented to the nearest National Institute of Health Insurance office (known as INAM/Instituto Nazionale per l'Assicurazione contro le Malattie). They will issue you with a certificate confirming the right to free treatment and, on request, supply a list of doctors attached to the INAM scheme. For drugs supplied, a partial payment is sometimes required. Otherwise, one is entitled to free treatment, either at home or at the surgery.

Bring your certificate to the chemist (farmacia) when having prescriptions filled. You need another certificate (proposta di recovero) for free hospital treatment, which should be issued by your doctor.

Specialist treatment and dental treatment are available at INAM surgeries and in hospitals and private clinics recognised by INAM. A list of these is also available from INAM. Payment for private treatment will be refunded to the sum normally paid to the public medical service for that treatment. The individual pays the difference. 'Pronto soccorso' are 24-hour emergency clinics at airports, ports, railway stations and in all hospitals, where they will attend to you without looking for forms.

LUXEMBOURG

Luxembourg is so tiny and the opportunities there so limited that it does not warrant a detailed discussion. French is the official language. Business is usually conducted in German and a patois, Luxembourgeois, is generally spoken.

The information in relation to EC countries in general holds good and the people seem to have a more positive attitude to working foreigners than some of their neighbours.

There is no embassy for Luxembourg in Ireland, but the embassy in London (see p. 111) can provide general information and addresses of companies and hotels that may be worth writing to. The national employment service (L'Administration de l'emploi) is available to EC members and young people can also avail of the State Youth Information Service (Service Nationale de la Jeunesse, see p. 119).

Most of the work available in Luxembourg seems to be of a casual kind, in hotels or factories. People with commercial or secretarial skills and good languages may have a chance of long-term work with the larger companies.

THE NETHERLANDS

BACKGROUND INFORMATION

Located on the North Sea, bordering Belgium and West Germany, the Netherlands has an area of 42,000 square kilometres and a population of over 14 million, with some 353 people per square kilometre — the highest population density in the EC. It has been a constitutional monarchy since 1848. The Hague is the centre of government, Amsterdam (population almost 1 million) the capital city. The monetary unit is the guilder, denoted by f, strangely enough (NLf3 = IR£1). The principal language is Dutch; English and German are also spoken. A knowledge of Dutch is very useful, but not absolutely essential for low-grade work. Dutch companies have been employing the best of Irish graduates for several years now, mostly computer engineering or science professionals. In other areas the work outlook is definitely not rosy and the official agencies are notably reluctant to part with any detailed information on work or official regulations.

VISAS AND PERMITS

No visa is required. For a stay of less than three months, an Irish national needs only a valid passport and sufficient means to cover his stay and return journey. Customs officials are empowered to enquire into your circumstances on arrival and they are very likely to do so. However, intending workers and those who wish to stay longer than three months must apply within eight days for a residence permit.

Everyone staying for any length of time, tourist or otherwise, is supposed to report to the Aliens Office within eight days of arrival in the country. Also, any foreigner who stays in any district for more than eight days is obliged to inform the local police. This formality is usually fulfilled by the management of the accommodation you are using. If you are staying privately, with friends, the onus is on you to report to the nearest police station.

A residence permit is issued to those who can provide either proof of employment (payslips or a contract), a definite (written) employment offer or possession of adequate funds and accommodation. It is a hazy area: official literature is no more specific than 'to obtain a residence permit one must fulfil certain conditions regarding accommodation and solvency.'

Residence permits are issued by the local aliens office (Vreemdelingenpolitie), if one exists in your area, or the police headquarters nearest your place of residence. Much is left to the discretion of the police officer conducting the interview. Be prepared for a discouraging attitude and be ready with information. Have your passport, some passport photographs and written proof of work or financial resources with you. A knowledge of Dutch is not essential, but it is useful for filling in forms and certainly makes a better impression.

Those intending to study also require a residence permit, if they stay for longer than three months. Students should provide proof of registration at a Dutch school or training institute, adequate finance for studies and living costs, and a health certificate.

WORK

The Dutch prefer you to have written confirmation of a job offer before leaving home, which is understandable in the light of their own fairly high level of unemployment (12% in 1986) and the recent tendency for Irish student workers to become stranded through factory or bulb-field failing to fulfil casual job offers. Writing for information from Ireland to the Dutch Ministry of Social Affairs and Employment (Ministerie van Sociale Zaken en Werkgelegenheid, see p. 120), as the Dutch Embassy's informative handout recommends, is unlikely to do much good — they will refer you back to FAS.

In fact, the Dutch are not at all welcoming to the casual foreign worker, having suffered rather an excess over recent years. There is work available, especially in food factories or the bulb industry. Long-term work is most often found from Ireland, especially in the large engineering and electronics companies. Popular daily newspapers are *Dagblad de Telegraaf* and *De Volkskrant* (Amsterdam) and *NRC Handelsblad* (Rotterdam).

Private employment agencies (Uitzendbureau) are more likely to be of use, especially for short-term jobs, than the State service (Arbeidsbureau). Two of the largest private companies are Randstad and Keser (see p. 120). The youth organisation (BIJK) can provide information on exchange programmes and au pairing.

For those interested in bulb-picking, a centralised agency (Koninklijke Algemene Vereniging voor Bloembollencultuur) can provide useful information (*see p. 120*). There are exchange and training schemes available for farmers and agriculturalists through the Foundation for Rural Exchange and Study Trips (Stichting Uitwisseling), for which membership of a farmer's or agricultural organisation in Ireland is first required. A similar farming agency is Landbouwschap.

For those interested in further education in a Dutch university or third-level institution, two scholarships are available each year to Irish graduates. NUFFIC (Netherlands University Foundation for International Cooperation) is a foundation for international exchange and collaboration among universities and technical institutions. It can provide information on courses in Holland and the value of specific diplomas abroad.

TAXATION

Income tax (Loonbelasting) and social insurance contributions are deducted from wages under the Netherlands' PAYE system. People who have worked for only a short period will not be entitled to rebates (unless they manage to fulfil residency requirements), since rebates can only be obtained through a tax declaration at the end of the fiscal year. Non-residents cannot make a tax declaration (return). Everyone, including students, has to pay tax.

HEALTH

Immediate free treatment should be provided with the E111. If necessary, contact the General Sickness Insurance Fund (ANOZ/ Algemeen Nederlands Onderling Ziekenfonds). Once working you have to register with a sickness fund and pay contributions.

GREECE, PORTUGAL AND SPAIN

These countries are relative newcomers to the EC and do not yet have to comply fully with the regulations on freedom of movement for workers.

Portugal and Spain (*see p. 90*) are entitled, and will be until 1993, to require a foreign worker to get advance authorisation from the migration authorities to work in either country. This is effectively a work visa, which has to be applied for in the home country on the basis of a formal job offer or contract.

The unrestricted movement of workers to **Greece** became effective in 1988. But to work in the country, you still need both a residence permit and a work permit, which should preferably be obtained before you go.

Portugal and Greece are two European countries which do not really rate a mention in a book about working overseas. There are very few opportunities in either country and wages are very low. They have surprisingly low unemployment rates (Portugal 8.4% and Greece just over 6% in 1986), but each has a large young population and there is little or no shortage of either skilled or unskilled labour. If there is a demand, local people fill it or an alternative supply of labour can readily be found, very cheaply, from neighbouring countries.

The lifestyles and climates of both countries are pleasant but, with the exception of work in the tourist industry (often very badly paid) or, in Greece, teaching English as a foreign language, there is little chance of sampling either apart from going there on holiday. In the long-term demand may increase, in the business, commercial and language areas, through the economic development which could come with EC membership.

From Ireland, teachers may find jobs in international schools and secretaries with languages may find openings. There is a remote chance of finding work in multinational companies, particularly for those with technological qualifications.

SPAIN

BACKGROUND INFORMATION

Spain has a population of over 38 million and an area of some 504,000 square kilometres. EC membership has created a huge upsurge in the demand for teachers of English. Otherwise, a very high unemployment rate (a fantastic 20.1% in 1988), combined with a highly qualified young population, means that Spain is capable of filling its needs in most areas of work. There is also an understandable preference for Spanish nationals on the part of employers.

Spain is similar to Italy in the extent to which European languages are spoken and there will be a definite need for language, commercial and secretarial skills as Europeanisation has its effect. Spain is unlike Italy, however, in that the country is well developed industrially and has a relatively stable economy, with inflation at around 5%. The cost of living is low by European standards. The currency is the Spanish peseta (SPp167 = IR£1). Besides the capital, Madrid (population 3.2 million), there are many regional population centres such as Barcelona (1.75 million), Malaga, Seville and Bilbao (880,000), giving a good spread of commercial and industrial activity all round the country.

VISAS AND PERMITS

The free movement of workers to Spain will not become effective until 1993. The visa and permit situation is complicated by a 7-year transitional period (from initial EC membership in 1986) during which the requirements of foreign workers have changed from time to time. The standard EC regulation, of needing only a valid passport for the first three months if you are a tourist, does, however, apply in Spain. But if you want to work there, study, or stay longer than three months, you must have a visa.

You need three official documents before you can work in Spain legally. First, you need to apply for a work visa to the Spanish Embassy in Dublin before you leave. For this, you must have written proof of a job offer. Second, you must have a work permit, which can be applied for either directly in Spain or through the

Embassy here, although the authorities prefer you to obtain the work permit, like the visa, before you go. And third, you need a residence permit, obtainable in Spain.

To get your visa, you have to supply the following documents to the Embassy in Dublin: a passport with at least 180 days' validity remaining, three passport photos and a written offer of employment, or precontract. The job offer is essential before a visa is issued. An application form is completed at the Embassy, photocopied and stamped. You have then to send this to Spain for the employer to apply for a work permit. When the employer has got the permit, the Embassy in Dublin notifies you and the visa is then issued. It is all rather complicated and long drawn out.

These rules do not apply to people who have already been working in Spain and had work permits issued before 1 January 1986. They can have both work and residence permits for 5 years according to EC regulations, even if the original permit issued was valid for a shorter period. Those who already have a work permit issued after 1 January 1986, valid for 12 months, are entitled to a further work and residence permit valid for 5 years.

In Spain itself, you can apply for a work permit (permiso de trabajo) directly from the issuing body (Ministerio de Trabajo y Seguridad Social) via the local provincial labour office (Direccion Provincial de Trabajo). The official list of documents required is lengthy and detailed. First, you are supposed to produce the initial visa or advance authorisation from the Embassy. Then you need a memorandum of the company; description of the position to be filled; photocopies of the first 5 pages of the applicant's passport already checked by the Embassy; visa granted by the Embassy on the basis of the application permit or employment contract; medical certificate already checked by the Embassy; 5 passport photos; work contract; certificate of good conduct; and finally, proof that the company has registered with the Spanish Social Security. By the way, you cannot have a legal employment contract unless you are over 18, or 16 if married.

It is unclear as to what happens officially if you enter Spain as a tourist, stay for 90 days and get a job offer. In this case, it may be possible to produce the other documentation for a work permit, including an employment contract, but not the initial visa authorisation (which, of course, you did not need as a tourist). Confusion in this area is rife. But the demand for English teachers, for example, especially in certain areas, makes Spanish schools very willing to oblige with whatever help they can in relation to the employee's work permit. The whole official process can be slow, even take several months, during which time it appears to be possible to work.

WORK

Teaching English as a foreign language is the major source of employment for foreigners in Spain. It is possible to apply for jobs from here — a rash of advertisements appears in the Irish newspapers at the beginning of each summer. *The Guardian* (Tuesdays) is a good source of advertisements, especially during July and August when schools are recruiting for the following academic year. Alternatively, the British Council offices in London, Madrid, Barcelona and Valencia can provide lists of language schools (*see p. 113, 120*). The major language school companies, such as Inlingua and Berlitz, operate numerous schools in Spain. Private tutoring is readily available and may be a better income-earner, although it requires some time to get established.

Tourism is a major industry in Spain and there is work available in various capacities. Tour guides and representatives with travel companies, hotel, restaurant, disco and bar staff (mostly very casual), people to promote and advertise tourist establishments, sales personnel of all types (including representatives to promote time-share apartments for property companies) — people are needed in all these areas, especially in the resorts of the Costa Brava, Costa Blanca and Costa del Sol on the Mediterranean coast. Irish and British tour companies who provide package holidays (apartment and camping) should be contacted as early in the season as possible (ie March/April, depending on the resort).

Au pair positions are readily available and Irish girls have traditionally been popular with Spanish families. The Spanish youth organisation, Instituto de la Juventud, coordinates workcamps in the country, many of which are archaeological or environmental conservation projects (*see p. 120*).

Finally, it is possible to put your command of the English language to use, especially if you also have good Spanish. Secretarial and translation services are provided by agencies or you can advertise yourself directly. University noticeboards may be a good source for more casual work of this nature — typing theses, etc.

TAXATION

Tax is unavoidable for anyone who spends more than 183 days in the year in Spain, which is the time period for residency. There is no double-taxation agreement between Ireland and Spain. Income tax is global, imposed on all income, and there are no special reliefs for foreign nationals who are resident in Spain. Income tax rates are, however, low by European standards, starting at about 25% for the average income, with wide bands and a maximum rate of 46%.

Everyone must pay social security contributions, which cover you for both medical care and unemployment benefit. Social security contributions and unemployment benefit will not be transferable until 1993.

HEALTH

Health care is provided for those with the E111. They can see a doctor at the local social security medical clinic. There is a minimum fee for prescriptions, even with the E111. Otherwise, the total cost must be paid.

Au pairs are not part of the official work system, but are considered as holiday workers and as such are not covered by social security. Private insurance cover is therefore recommended.

6
Non-EC European Countries

These countries have one thing in common — they all have work to offer. Most of them are also quite inaccessible for the outsider who wants to work legally. Turkey is an exception: it is relatively welcoming to the foreign worker and as a developing country its salaries and cost of living are low. The others — Austria, Switzerland and all three Scandinavian countries (Finland, Norway and Sweden) — are economically strong, have high living costs, low unemployment rates and are difficult to get into.

From the following outline of the work-visa requirements for each country, you will see the similarities in the kind of immigration policy they all pursue. They fully regulate the movement of workers and migrants must, in most cases, have a job arranged and a work visa before entering the country. There is often a further requirement for both a residence and a work permit, issued either before entry on the basis of the job offer or in the country after entry with a work visa. All of the regulations work on the basis of a specific position and with the cooperation of the employer.

There are some official schemes that can provide chances of experiencing the work situation in these countries; this way, you may get a foot in the door. But, be warned: access is limited for the most part to highly skilled professionals, who are in demand in certain fields such as science, engineering and electronics, or to the practically trained, including tradespeople and those in agriculture or horticulture, or to those already trained in some aspect of the hotel and catering trade. Most of these countries cooperate with official training programmes and international work experience schemes, such as the work visas for the 'stage' trainee scheme (*see p. 31*). They also cooperate with organisations for students such as IAESTE and AIESEC (*see p. 31*).

Of course, there is unlimited potential if you can persuade an employer in any of these destinations to take you on, independently, from this end. This is particularly true for the highly qualified or experienced in the areas of work mentioned above. A direct approach to an employer, who has to be willing to make a definite job offer and to help get a work permit, is the only route into most of these countries, apart from official schemes. Independent travel on spec is discouraged, since it is quite difficult to bypass the permit requirements, especially in the stricter Scandinavian countries. Switzerland and Austria are somewhat easier. There is, however, some seasonal or casual work available in most of these countries, in both hotels and agricultural occupations such as bulb-picking. Some countries — Sweden, for example — will issue students with temporary summer work visas, if they have a job arranged.

AUSTRIA

BACKGROUND INFORMATION

Austria has a population of 7.6 million and occupies an area of some 84,000 square kilometres. It shares borders with Czechoslovakia, Hungary, Yugoslavia, Italy, Switzerland and West Germany. Foreign trade and worker migration have traditionally been with Austria's Eastern European neighbours, but developing European orientation will result in an increased demand in the secretarial/marketing/financial management areas. An application for EC membership from Austria is expected during the summer of 1989.

The capital is Vienna (population almost 2 million). Other major cities are Linz, Graz, Salzburg and Innsbruck, the latter being the centre of the Tyrolean resort area. The language is German and a good command of it is essential, since relatively little English or French is spoken.

The currency is the Austrian schilling (ASs18 = IR£1) which is relatively stable. The unemployment rate has risen steadily during the '80s (5.2% in 1986), which explains the overtly discouraging attitude of the Austrian Embassy in Ireland. To quote their form letter, entitled *Job Opportunities in Austria*, 'The Austrian Embassy would like to point out that due to the present economic conditions it is generally difficult for foreign nationals to find employment in Austria.'

VISAS AND PERMITS

Austria has a working visa system similar to that operating in Switzerland (*see p. 104*). The employer has to get a work permit (Arbeitsbewilligüng) for the prospective employee before he can enter the country. Once the work permit has been obtained in Austria, the prospective employee has to apply at the Austrian Embassy in Ireland for a working visa.

The Austrian system differs from that of Switzerland in that the regional labour exchanges (Landesarbeitsaemter) control the issue of work permits to employers. They are entitled to refuse a work permit if there is a local person available who is suitable for the job. Au pairs are also required to obtain work permits before entering the country.

WORK

You can look for work from this end by writing directly to employers and regional labour exchanges in Austria. Fluent German and professional skills are most likely to meet with a response. The Austrian Embassy in Ireland can provide a list of suitable addresses (*see also p. 121*). The Irish Society in Vienna and the Anglo-Austrian Society in London are both good sources to tap (*see p. 121*).

Temporary work is also available, mostly in hotels which have traditionally used foreign (student) labour. The regional labour exchanges do not deal with temporary or au pair positions, so it is necessary to write directly to hotels or agencies. The local tourist offices in resort areas (such as Kitzbühel, Innsbruck and Mayrhofen) will provide lists of hotel addresses and are reputed to act as informal employment exchanges. Temporary and au pair work is not automatically covered by the social security and health schemes, therefore contributions are not always automatically deducted from pay.

Officially, there is no way of applying for a work permit once inside the country, but there are sometimes labour shortages, especially in the tourist industry and hoteliers may not be overly concerned about work permit regulations. Wages are low by Swiss or Scandinavian standards.

There are other agencies which organise voluntary work and workcamps in Austria, many of which are run by religious groups *(see p. 114)*. It is relatively easy to get a Volunteer Work Permit, which officially restricts the holder to a maximum monthly wage (approximately ASs3000 in 1988). People seeking au pair work can write to a number of agencies, including Arbeitsgemeinschaft Auslänrds-Sozialdienst — Au-Pair Vermittlung *(see p. 115)*. There is also an organisation, OEKISTA, which provides information for young people about temporary work and au pair openings. Among the places to offer further information, according to the Austrian Embassy in Dublin, is the 'Desk for Irish student exchange' at the Irish Embassy in Vienna *(see p. 121)*.

Official information for teachers emphasises that jobs in State schools are available only to those proficient in German and are reserved for Austrian citizens. Vacancies for teaching positions in State schools are advertised in the newspaper *Wiener Zeitung* on 1 May and 1 July each year; you can get a subscription to it from Ireland *(see p. 122)*. Applications and enquiries can also be sent to the local education authority of each province *(see p. 121)*.

The Austrian Embassy in Dublin suggest that teachers try the international schools, of which there are several in Vienna. It may also be possible for prospective teachers to get work on language assistantships. Teachers and activity leaders are also recruited each summer for language camps run by an organisation called Osterreichische Jugendferienwerk in Salzburg *(see p. 121)*.

S C A N D I N A V I A
FINLAND, NORWAY AND SWEDEN

The Nordic countries (Sweden, Denmark, Norway, Finland and Iceland) have a common labour market policy which allows free movement of workers between their countries. Immigration is otherwise fully regulated, with the exception of Denmark which must (however reluctantly) allow entry to its fellow EC members *(see pp. 69-72)*. In each of the others, the foreign worker must have a specific, pre-arranged job to come to and a permit to work.

The Irish person is not only up against the difficulty of finding work from afar, but also is competing with the entire Nordic labour force, which has the advantage of mutually intelligible languages and unrestricted access. The unemployment figures are impressive: in 1986 only 2.5% of the Swedish population was unemployed, in Norway 2.0%, in Finland 5.4%, in Denmark 8.0% and in Iceland 1.2% (1984).

In all of these countries, an Irish person must find a job; then the employer must apply to the labour market board to assess the local situation. Official Swedish literature states, 'In principle, work permits are only awarded in exceptional cases where labour has proved unobtainable in any other way.'

The application for a work permit to the relevant embassy in Ireland must include a concrete and plausible written offer of employment on a special form. The employer must also provide a statement from the labour market board. The foreign worker must also get a residence permit and anyone, tourist or otherwise, must get a permit to stay longer than three months.

The outlook for obtaining a work permit in this manner is grim: Sweden, for example, issues only about 100 a year. Norway has until recently been a little more accessible. Although there has been an official ban in Norway on non-Nordic immigration since 1975, exceptions have been made for highly skilled professionals in certain areas — mostly engineering and science — which were suffering local shortages. Student vacation-workers and those looking for work-experience opportunities are most likely to find openings in Finland. Sweden also offers summer work permits to students.

The one major exception to these strict visa regulations is the availability of work permits for experience programmes under bilateral agreements for international exchange. These permits are usually based on quotas and considered exempt from local labour market demands. This category includes not only those on official programmes for work experience (such as those run by IAESTE, AIESEC and FAS), but also people who work in areas where needs and demands for a workforce may be thought to have an international basis. In Sweden, for example, this category includes managerial and specialised personnel employed by international companies which, as part of their normal activities, have an acceptable need for temporary employment within a company in Sweden. It also includes research scientists, certain artists and qualified cooks for restaurants of international standard (as well as trainees under exchange agreements and those on official post-qualifying work experience).

Work permits issued under this category are usually specifically limited in terms of duration, occupation and employer. They are normally valid for 12 to 18 months, with a maximum duration of 24 months.

FINLAND (SF)

BACKGROUND INFORMATION

Finland has an area of 337,000 square kilometres and a population of 4.9 million. The population density is low, with 15 inhabitants per square kilometre. Most Finns live in the southern coastal region, while the far north (Lappland) is sparsely populated. The people have a reputation for great friendliness and hospitality. The capital is Helsinki (population 483,000); the only other major city and port is Turku (163,000). Lahti and Hämeenlinna are popular resorts in the lakes area north of Helsinki. Lappland, in the extreme north, is developing a tourist trade with Lemmenjoki, a major centre.

The language is Finnish, which is similar to the other Scandinavian languages. Finland has traditionally been rather a poor relation in Scandinavian terms and there is a tradition of worker migration, principally to Sweden. The currency is the Finnish markka (Fm6.22 = IR£1).

VISAS AND PERMITS

Finland cooperates with many international exchange programmes and it is official policy to encourage intercultural exchange. So it is possible to get there both for short periods of temporary work or cultural exchange — usually during the summer — and for longer work experience programmes, of up to 18 months. This access is not limited to the professionally qualified; there are openings for practical or vocational trades, too. You do, however, usually have to have completed some specific qualification or training. Many of the programmes are in the work areas of agriculture or horticulture. IAESTE, AFS — Interculture Ireland and FAS can provide information on schemes they run (see p. 112). In Finland, the Ministry of Labour's International Trainee Exchanges Division organises these programmes in cooperation with IAESTE and their office may also provide information (*see p. 122*).

International exchange programmes excepted, work and residence permits are rarely issued, as in other Scandinavian countries. When they are, it is usually only on the basis that no Finn is available to do the job in question. Permits must be obtained before you enter the country. Both a work permit and a residence permit are required, the former usually being granted for a period of three months, after which it must be extended.

WORK

Professionals, such as architects, engineers and computer personnel, may find openings. Agriculture and fishing, including mariculture, are other major sources of employment, though non-Nordics are most likely to gain access to these areas through exchange programmes. Seasonal work does exist in the flower industry (for which the Helsinki area is a major centre), especially at picking time in August and September. Fully qualified teachers, with good EFL training, may get year-long contracts for English teaching in secondary schools. This is organised by the Finnish-British Society, which can be contacted through the British Council in London (*see p. 113*). There are also opportunities for language assistantships and short-term tutoring.

NORWAY

BACKGROUND INFORMATION

Norway is the fifth largest country in Europe, with an area of some 325,000 square kilometres and an extensive coastline (2750 km), mostly on the North and Norwegian Seas. Sweden, Finland and the USSR provide land borders. Despite its great size, Norway's population is only 4.2 million, giving a density of 13 inhabitants per square kilometre — the least densely populated country in Europe.

Bergen (population 208,000), Stavanger, Drammen and Oslo, the capital (643,000), are major urban centres of the south.

Kristiansund and Trondheim (135,000) are cities and major ports in the south-east. English is widely spoken throughout Norway.

Norway's traditional industries were fisheries and forestry (with allied timber, paper and pulp production). However, rich oil and mineral resources have become the mainstay of economic expansion — especially since the discovery of major oil deposits in the North Sea in the early '70s. Norway has developed major electro-metallurgical and electro-chemical industries, as well as shipbuilding and oilrig technology. The steel industry, based on rich iron ore resources, is largely State-owned. Economic development is steady and Norwegians enjoy a high standard of living, though inflation is relatively high (8.9% in 1987). The currency is the Norwegian krone (Nkr9.74 = IR£1).

VISAS AND PERMITS

Although there is a Norwegian Embassy in Dublin, it is difficult to find out about the work permit situation in this country. Visa regulations are just as strict as those in Sweden. A job and suitable accommodation must be arranged before applying for a visa. A work permit must then be approved before the Embassy in Ireland will issue a visa. It will only be approved on the basis that no national is available for the job in question. Once in the country, a residence permit is required, issued by the local police.

Norway does not appear to have a visa programme for summer vacation work, although it did until 1984. They are not as involved in trainee exchange programmes as the Finns and, generally, do not appear to welcome the foreign worker — at least not those who make enquiries as to the specific work permits and visa regulations at the Embassy here in Ireland. There is a Farm Guest Programme run by the Norwegian Youth Council. It aims to provide experience of farming life for periods of between 1 and 3 months to those aged between 18 and 30. Pocket money is provided (*see p. 122*).

WORK

Apart from highly specialised aspects of oil exploitation, engineering and metallurgy, few opportunities are apparent in Norway. It may, however, be possible to find seasonal work. Fisheries (canning and processing) employ large numbers of casual staff, as does small-scale agricultural production. The tourist industry is probably more accessible to the foreign worker. Try writing from here to hotels (addresses are obtainable from the Norwegian Tourist Office in London, *see p. 122*).

SWEDEN

BACKGROUND INFORMATION

Like the other Scandinavian countries, Sweden has a small population, with about 8.4 million people living in an area of 450,000 square kilometres. This gives a density of only 20 inhabitants for each square kilometre. But 83% of the population is concentrated in the urban areas of the south, principally in the capital Stockholm (population 1.4 million) and in the ports of Malmö (453,000) and Gothenburg (694,000).

Sweden is governed by the one chamber parliament, the Riksdag, where the Social Democrats have been in power, either alone or in coalition, since 1932, except for a shaky period from 1976 to 1982 when the non-socialist parties held office.

There is a strong welfare state and a huge public sector, with nearly one in three of employed people working for the State in some capacity. There are also many State-owned companies, including 10% of the business sector. There were about 40,000 immigrants in Sweden in 1986 and migrant workers and refugees comprise around 4.7% of the total population. Most of these are Finns, but there are also surprisingly large numbers of Iranians and Asians. During the 1960s and early '70s, Sweden accepted many migrant workers from other European countries, including Yugoslavia, Greece and Turkey.

Taxes and living costs are high in Sweden, as in all the Scandinavian countries. The currency is the Swedish krone (SEk9.16 = IR£1). Inflation is around 5% and 40% of the average income of a typical full-time worker goes in direct taxation. There are both State and local taxes. VAT rates are very high. Employees also contribute to both the social security system, which covers health care (only in part) and provides sickness benefit, and to unemployment funds (arbetsförmedlingen), which are mostly organised by trades unions.

VISAS AND PERMITS

In order to get a work permit, the prospective employee must apply to the Swedish Embassy in Dublin, with a special form provided by the employer which details the job offer (and includes provision of adequate accommodation). The employer may have obtained advance approval prior to recruitment from the Labour Market Board. In this case, he will also provide a statement of prior notification. Failing this, the case will be referred to the Immigration Board which, in turn, will request approval from the Labour Market Board. Approval is extremely unlikely unless it is an exceptional case and you are required (and qualified) for a key position.

Residence permits must also be obtained before entering the country. As the Embassy literature states, 'Non-Nordic citizens have very little chance of entering Sweden as migrant workers.'

There are, however, ways of getting into Sweden. If you are a student, you can get a vacation work permit. Alternatively, you can join an international exchange programme or apply for a period of post-qualifying work experience. Sweden operates bilateral agreements for the latter with 8 countries, including Ireland.

WORK

Employment opportunities are limited for the most part to technological and scientific industries. Pharmaceuticals and biotechnology are major growth areas and there are some large Swedish companies involved in engineering and electronics that are almost household names, among them Ericsson, Volvo and Electrolux.

Recruitment programmes are conducted from time to time in Britain for English teachers for State-run adult language programmes in the Folk University of Sweden (see p. 122). There may also be work available in hotels and food-processing factories. Voluntary workcamps are another possible means of legal entry to Sweden (see p. 122).

Students can try to find work in these areas, but they must apply for vacation work permits. The permits last for a total period of three months, anytime between 15 May and 15 October, and are available to those aged under 30 on 15 May of the year of intended employment. A quota is set annually by the county employment boards for different occupations and areas. Each permit issued takes one place in the quota. A job offer has first to be obtained, then you must apply at least eight weeks before the proposed date of entry, with a certificate showing your continuing enrolment in an educational establishment and proof from your employer that housing has been arranged for you, as well as form AMS PF 1704 which the employer must have had approved by the county employment board in Sweden. Of course, the major difficulty is to find an employer from this end. The Irish Society in Sweden may be able to help (*see p. 122*).

SWITZERLAND (CH)

BACKGROUND INFORMATION

Switzerland's location and economic emphasis on small-scale quality of service or product rather than mass production, together with services such as banking and insurance, has made its almost 6.5 million inhabitants among the wealthiest in Europe. The population density is 157 per square kilometre. Switzerland's 41,293 square kilometres are mountainous and completely land-locked, but borders with Italy, France, Austria and the Federal Republic of Germany result in a multilingual society. Although the majority of the population (73.5%) speak German, 20.1% speak French, and a minority (4.5%) in the southern regions speak Italian. Many people speak both French and German, as well as English; all are used for business and commercial purposes. Berne (population 138,600) is the federal capital; Zürich (400,000) and Geneva (160,000) are other major centres.

The political system consists of a federation of 26 cantons, each with their own constitutions, governments and courts, and separate administration for tax, social welfare and other systems. This cantonal system means that regulations are not completely uniform, though they are similar in effect. The federal authorities, however, supervise migration and the ultimate legal authority is held by the federal court. There were 940,000 foreigners living in Switzerland in 1986, many of whom were migrant workers from Italy and Austria. The Swiss franc is strong (Sfr2.27 = IR£1), inflation around 3% and unemployment almost non-existent — under 1% (0.8) in 1986. The cost of food and and accommodation is among the highest in Europe, although people employed in a surprising number of occupations, including butchers, gardeners and bakers, are usually provided with room and board.

VISAS AND PERMITS

You need a valid passport and a provisional assurance of a residence permit (assurance d'autorisation de séjour *or* zusicherung der aufenthaltsbewilligüng) to enter the country to work legally. This means you have to find an employer who is prepared to offer you a job and then to go through the local authorities for a provisional assurance on your behalf. This provisional assurance form has to be obtained by the prospective employer from the cantonal authorities and sent to you outside the country. The employer must also provide an employment contract. You can then enter the country and apply for a residence permit.

Irish citizens do not actually need a visa, but the provisional assurance fulfils a similar function. Tourists can, however, stay for up to three months without a permit, though nationals of some countries (not Ireland) need entry visas. Foreigners intending to take up employment in Switzerland also have to register with the local Aliens Police within eight days of arrival in the country.

Everyone intending to work has to have a medical check for 'communicable disease' at a frontier health control centre when entering the country. These are closed on Saturdays, Sundays and statutory holidays, and only open for limited periods the rest of the time, when queues can stretch waiting time to far more than two or three hours.

Once you are working, the full residence permit (autorisation de séjour) is issued according to the provisional assurance given to the employer and on the basis of the original job you were offered. A change of jobs may be authorised after the first year, but a change to another profession or work area, or canton, is usually prohibited during the first three years.

It may, unofficially, be possible to enter as a tourist and then apply for a residence permit inside the country, when you find an employer. However, official literature states that applications for residence permits from people inside the country are not considered until at least a month after their departure.

WORK

'Stages' (traineeships): It is possible to apply for work experience with companies, especially in the service industries, and enter Switzerland as a trainee (stagiare). The 'stage' scheme is organised by agreement between the relevant authorities (in Ireland, the Department of Labour) and is available for a number of different occupations. The aim is to provide further education and occupational training through a stay abroad. Trainees must have completed their vocational training, be between 18 and 30 years of age and wish to gain experience in their own field. The occupations pursued are dictated, obviously, by the applicant's training, but include anything except those from which foreigners are prohibited in Switzerland, such as law, pharmacy, dentistry, veterinary surgery and medicine, which are usually reserved for Swiss citizens.

Work permits for 'stages' are usually issued for one year, extended in rare cases to 18 months. The scheme is not available to apprentices, domestic servants, semi-skilled and unskilled workers, or students. The Irish Committee for the Exchange of Stagiares with Foreign Countries, at the Department of Labour, can provide further information.

Au pairs must obtain a residence permit in the official way, with a contract and a provisional assurance. They are strictly regulated, have to be between 17 and 29, attend language classes twice a week and must intend to stay (usually) for a minimum of one year. There are minimum salary levels and working hours.

From this end: The Embassy here issues a page of information for people wishing to work in Switzerland, which recommends placing an advertisement in a newspaper to find a position. There is an agency in England that will organise insertions and translations of ads in the chosen papers (*see p. 123*). Hotel work can be applied for through the Swiss Hotel Association's Staff Bureau (*see p. 122*). Applications should be detailed and experience and languages help the chances of finding a position. People employed in agriculture or hotels and restaurants are usually provided with room and board. The tourist industry can provide openings; Jobs in the Alps and Vacation Work International are two British agencies that can help organise work and permits (*see p. 122*).

TAXATION

In Switzerland, there are income tax payments for the federal authorities and local (cantonal or communal) taxes. Foreign workers usually have their tax deducted at source by the employer. In theory, a tax declaration is completed every two years and liability decided on this basis. For the short-term worker, the employer usually decides rates. Tax rates are progressive and similar to Britain's, or slightly lower.

HEALTH

Accident insurance is compulsory for all workers and is deducted from the pay packet, along with social insurance contributions for pensions. Everyone should also join a private health insurance scheme, though membership of such schemes is not compulsory in all parts of Switzerland. The insurance should include medical and hospital treatment and sickness benefit, since payment of wages in the event of illness is usually limited. The Bundesamt für Sozialversicherung in Berne can give advice and further information (*see p. 122*).

TURKEY

BACKGROUND INFORMATION

Turkey occupies an area of 780,580 square kilometres. The total population is approximately 34 million and increasing rapidly. Istanbul is the principal city, though the capital is Ankara. Other major cities include Izmir, Bursa, Çanakkale and Muğla. Many areas along the Aegean coast are developing rapidly into tourist centres, including the towns of Kuşadasi, Marmaris and Fethiye. The currency is the Turkish lira (T*l* 1500 = IR£1). Turkey shares borders with Greece, Bulgaria, the USSR, Iran, Iraq and Syria. The language is Turkish, though a surprising amount of English is spoken, especially in the cities such as Istanbul, Izmir and the tourist resorts of the Aegean.

Turkey occupies a unique position between Europe and Asia,

and suffers many of the problems of a Third World country in terms of development, while adopting a pro-European, pro-EC policy. Inflation, unemployment and low standards of living are major problems. Illiteracy is high, especially in rural areas and among women. The political system is oppressive and relatively unstable, and while Turkey is by no means as strict or fanatical as its Arab neighbours, religion has an effect on the opportunities and lifestyle available to women workers. It is, however, an interesting and varied country in which to gain work experience. The people have a reputation for friendliness and hospitality. Low pay levels relate to a low cost of living, though many jobs provide accommodation or assistance with rent as a result of high accommodation costs, especially in Istanbul.

VISAS AND PERMITS

No visa is required for visits of up to three months. In order to work, however, a working visa is required. This should be applied for before entry. A position must be found and an application should then be made to the Embassy here, who will then apply to the relevant Turkish authority for a work permit. A visa will be issued when the authorities have approved the work permit.

An employer may also apply directly for a work permit in Turkey, in which case approval for the visa will be sent to the Embassy which may then grant the visa. The visa application must include a passport and photographs, a completed visa application form, a signed and sealed copy of the employment contract and a letter from the employer detailing the type of work to be undertaken and the location at which the applicant will be based.

It appears to be possible to apply for a work permit within the country, with the aid of an employer, though the official position is otherwise. There are International Student and Training Exchange schemes for which a visa and working permit are also required.

WORK

There is a need in Turkey for many kinds of skills and expertise. There are opportunities within the tourist industry, with travel firms as guides and representatives, in hotels and in sales and marketing companies catering for the tourist trade. Engineering and technical personnel are needed for development projects (vacancies are usually advertised overseas by State-contracted companies).

Teachers of English can find work everywhere, especially in the numerous language schools and third-level technical institutions of Istanbul. There are also some openings in language teaching in universities, notably the American University in Izmir.

The organisations that deal with Turkey are mostly British-based. It is difficult to get information from the Embassy in Ireland on either work opportunities or even the visa and work permit regulations. The international exchange organisations, workcamp agencies and recruitment agencies (such as the British Council, CBEVE and UNA, *see p. 113, 114*) are the most likely sources of specific opportunities.

7
Useful Addresses

EMBASSIES AND CONSULAR MISSIONS FOR EUROPE

AUSTRIA: 15 Ailesbury Court, 93 Ailesbury Road, Dublin 4. Tel: 694577, 691451.

BELGIUM: Shrewsbury House, Shrewsbury Road, Dublin 4. Tel: 692082, 691588.

DENMARK: 121 St Stephens Green, Dublin 2. Tel: 756404 (hours: 9.00-16.30).

FINLAND: 11 Carnegielaan, 2517 KH, The Hague, Netherlands. Tel: 469754.

Honorary Consul-General: J. Donnelly, Fitzwilton House, Wilton Place, Dublin 2. Tel: 765153.

FRANCE: 36 Ailesbury Road, Dublin 4. Tel: 694777 (hours: 9.00-12.30).

GERMANY: 31 Trimleston Avenue, Booterstown, Co. Dublin. Tel: 693011 (hours: 9.00-12.00).

GREECE: 1 Upper Pembroke Street, Dublin 2. Tel: 767254.

ITALY: 63 Northumberland Road, Dublin 4. Tel: 601744.

LUXEMBOURG: 27 Wilton Crescent, London SW1X 8SD. Tel: 235 6961.

Honorary Consul-General: M. Murphy, 21 Deerpark Drive, Dublin 15. Tel: 212497.

THE NETHERLANDS: 160 Merrion Road, Dublin 4. Tel: 693444 (hours: 10.00-12.30, 14.20-16.00).

NORWAY: Hainault House, 69 St Stephens Green, Dublin 2. Tel: 783133 (hours: 9.00-16.00).

PORTUGAL: Knocknasinna House, Foxrock, Dublin 18. Tel: 894416.

SPAIN: 17a Merlyn Park, Dublin 4. Tel: 691640, 692597.

SWEDEN: PO Box 1313, Sun Alliance House, 13-17 Dawson Street, Dublin 2. Tel: 715822 (hours: 9.30-12.30).

SWITZERLAND: 6 Ailesbury Road, Dublin 4. Tel: 692515.

TURKEY: 60 Merrion Road, Dublin 4. Tel: 685240.

Turkish Consulate: Rutland Lodge, Rutland Gardens, Knightsbridge, London SW7 1BW.

OFFICIAL ORGANISATIONS, AGENCIES AND GOVERNMENT DEPARTMENTS IN IRELAND, UK AND EUROPE

AFS — Interculture Ireland, 29 Lower Baggot Street, Dublin 2. Tel: 762027 (Young Worker Programme).

AIESEC (International Association for Students of Economics and Management), UKIN House, Phipp Street, London EC2A 4NR.

Department of Education, Ceann Oifig 2, Marlborough Street, Dublin 1. Tel: 717101 (language assistantships and scholarships).

Department of Foreign Affairs (Development Cooperation Division), 76-78 Harcourt Street, Dublin 2. Tel: 780822.

Department Of Health, European Information Unit, Custom House, Dublin 1. Tel: 735777.

Department of Labour, Davitt House, Mespil Road, Dublin 4. Tel: 765861 (the exchange of 'stagiares' with foreign countries and SEDOC).

Department of Social Welfare, Aras Mhic Dhiarmada, Store Street, Dublin 1. Tel: 786444.

EC Control: European and International Information Section (*above address,* for general information and leaflet series);

EC Records Office, Gandon House, Amiens Street, Dublin 1. Tel: 786444 (for E301 and E104 record of contribution forms);

European Information Unit, 157 Townsend Street, Dublin 2. Tel: 786444 (for E303 and E106 transfer of benefit forms).

FAS, 27-33 Upper Baggot Street, Dublin 2. Tel: 685777 (Young Worker Exchange Programmes; Overseas Sponsorship; international work experience and training).

IAESTE (International Association for the Exchange of Students for Technical Experience), Honorary Secretary, Engineering School, University College Dublin, Upper Merrion Street, Dublin 2. Tel: 761584.

NARC (National Academic Recognition Information Centre), c/o Higher Education Authority, 21 Fitzwilliam Square, Dublin 2. Tel: 761545.

RIA (Royal Irish Academy), 19 Dawson Street, Dublin 2. Tel: 762570.

YEB, 10 Lower Hatch Street, Dublin 2. Tel: 618738 (Youth for Europe — EC exchanges and study visits for youth groups and youth leaders; International Fund for Ireland's Wider Horizons Programme — work experience and training in Europe, USA and Canada; French language assistantships in Canada; Young Workers Exchange Programmes; post-leaving certificate Voluntary Social Work Year in Germany; home-stay exchange programmes; school-link service and pre-leaving certificate term exchanges; language and group leader training; library with audio-visual resources and exchange database).

USIT, Aston Quay, O'Connell Bridge, Dublin 2. Tel: 778117 (Student travel organisation; also sells ISIC and YIEE cards and a wide range of maps, guides and jobs directories; 15% discount for holders of above cards. 14 offices around Ireland).

An Oige, 39 Mountjoy Square, Dublin 1. Tel: 363111 (Irish Youth Hostels Association).

INFORMATION SOURCES

Dublin Central Library, ILAC Centre, Dublin 1. Tel: 734333.

Dublin CYIC (Community and Youth Information Centre), Sackville House, Sackville Place, Dublin 1. Tel: 786844.

EC Information Office, 39 Molesworth Street, Dublin 2. Tel: 712244.

The British Council (Overseas Educational Appointments Department), 65 Davies Street, London W1Y 2AA.

CBEVE (The Central Bureau for Educational Visits and Exchanges), Seymour Mews House, Seymour Mews, London W1H 9PE.

ERICYA Secretariat, 101 quai Branly, F-75740 Paris, Cedex 15, France (central office for further information on ERICYA and its activities).

The Commission of the European Communities, DVG/C, rue de la Loi 200, B-1049, Brussels, Belgium (for further information on all EC initiatives, including Youth for Europe, ERASMUS and COMETT programmes).

VOLUNTARY SERVICE, DEVELOPMENT AND WORKCAMP ORGANISATIONS

APSO (Agency for Personal Service Overseas), 29 Fitzwilliam Square, Dublin 2. Tel: 614411.

VSI (Voluntary Service International), 4 Eustace Street, Dublin 2. Tel: 719067.

Comhchairdeas (Irish Workcamp Movement), 2 Belvedere Place, Dublin 1. Tel: 729681.

UNA (United Nations Association), International Service, Welsh Centre for International Affairs, Temple of Peace, Cathays Park, Cardiff CF1 3AP, Wales.

QWC (Quaker Workcamps), Friends House, Euston Road, London NW1 2BJ.

CMP (Christian Movement for Peace), Bethnal Green United Reform Church, Pott Street, London EC2.

Internationaler Bauorden, Postfach 770, 6520 Worms, FRG.

EMPLOYMENT AGENCIES

European Employment Consultants (EEC), 31 Castleknock Drive, Dublin 15. Tel: 204455 (professionals and executives).

Santos Engineering Services, 19 Clanwilliam Square, Dublin 2. Tel: 619911 (engineering and construction personnel).

Worldwide Recruitment, 3 Cathal Brugha Street, Dublin 1. Tel: 726130 (construction and trades personnel).

O'Grady Peyton International, Callaghan House, 13-16 Dame Street, Dublin 2. Tel: 779716 (medical, teaching, professional and clerical personnel).

PARC Recruitment Consultants, St John's Court, Swords Road, Dublin 9. Tel: 429933 (professional, medical and marketing personnel).

The Accountants Panel, 97 Lower Baggot Street, Dublin 2. Tel: 614771 (accountants and financial executives).

CSR (Computer Staff Recruitment) Consultants, Matrix House, 52 Lower Camden Street, Dublin 2. Tel: 783166 (computer programmers, analysts, operators and sales personnel, word-processing and data entry personnel).

Head Hunt (International Recruitment), Chatham House, Chatham Street, Dublin 2. Tel: 794733 (computer, electronics, engineering, accountancy, marketing and secretarial personnel).

CCM Recruitment International, McInerney Building, Old Naas Road, Bluebell, Dublin 12. Tel: 502922 (nurses and medical personnel).

Lansdowne International Services, 37 Golden Square, London W1R 4AL.

International Training and Recruitment Link, 13-14 Hanover Street, London W1R 9HG.

Elan Computing, The Old Forge Business Centre, 7 Caledonian Road, London N1 9DX.

Skilled Compupeople, Finland House, 56 Haymarket, London SW1Y 4RS.

Gabbitas Truman Thring, Broughton House, 6 Sackville Street, London W1X 2BR.

AU PAIR AGENCIES

IN IRELAND

Dublin School of English, 11 Westmoreland Street, Dublin 2. Tel: 773221.

International Study Centre, 67 Harcourt Street, Dublin 2. Tel: 782766.

Langcom, 37 Merrion Avenue, Blackrock, Co Dublin. Tel: 832349.

Linguaviva Centre, 45 Lower Leeson Street, Dublin 2. Tel: 789384.

The Language Centre, 9-11 Grafton Street, Dublin 2. Tel: 716266.

IN UK

Baxters Agency, PO Box 12, Peterborough, Cambs PE3 6JN.

Euro Employment Centre, 42 Upper Union Arcade, Bury, Lancs BL9 0QF.

Jolaine Agency, 171 High Street, Barnet, Herts EN5 5SU.

Helping Hands, 10 Hertford Road, Newbury Park, Ilford, Essex IG2 7HQ.

FOR AUSTRIA

OEKISTA, Türkenstrasse 4, A-1090 Vienna.

Arbeitsgemeinschaft Ausländs-Sozialdenst, Au-Pair Vermittlung, Johangasse 16, A-1010 Vienna.

FOR BELGIUM
AHOY Travel (au pair service), Anselmostraat 76, 2018 Antwerp.
Association des Services de la Jeunesse Féminine, rue Faider 29,
1050 Brussels.

FOR FRANCE
Séjours Internationaux Linguistiques et Culturels, 32 rempart de
l'Est, 16022 Angoulème Cedex.
Accueil Familial des jeunes étrangers, 23 rue du Cherche Midi,
75006 Paris.
Inter-Séjours, 4 rue de Parme, 75009 Paris.

FOR GERMANY
Verein für Internationale Jugendarbeit, 39 Craven Road, London
W2 3BX.
In Via (Deutscher Verband Katholischer Mädchensozialarbeit),
Postfach 420, 7800 Freiburg, FRG.

FOR ITALY
Au Pairs Italy, 46 The Rise, Sevenoaks, Kent TN13 1RJ.

FOR THE NETHERLANDS
BIJK (Bureau Internationale Jongeren Kontakten), Postbus 15344,
1001 MH Amsterdam.

FOR SPAIN
Asociacion Internacional Cultural Au Pair, Passeig de Gracia 86,
08008 Barcelona.
SAS Internacional, Rodríguez San Pedro 5,4.izq., 28015 Madrid.
Relaciones Culturales Internacionales, Ferraz 82,2., 28008 Madrid.

FOR SCANDINAVIA (among others)
Students Abroad, Elm House, 21b The Avenue, Hatch End,
Middlesex HA5 4EN.

FOR SWITZERLAND
Pro Filia, 14B avenue du Mail, 1205 Geneva.
Verein der Freundinnen Junger Mädchen, Zähringerstrasse 36,
8001 Zürich.

ADDRESSES FOR EC COUNTRIES

BELGIUM

State Employment Service: ONEM, rue d'Escalier 38, 1000 Brussels. ONEM, boulevard Anspach 65, 1000 Brussels. (This office includes a temporary job section 'T-service').

Youth Information Centres (Infor Jeunes and JAC): Centre Nationale Infor Jeunes (CNIJ), rue Traversière 4, 1030 Brussels. Infor Jeunes Bruxelles, rue Marché-aux-Herbes 27, 1000 Brussels. Info Jeugd Nationaal, Prinsstraat 15, 2000 Antwerp.

British Council: avenue Galilée-Galileilaan 5 (Bte 10), 1030 Brussels.

Irish Embassy: rue de Luxembourg 19, 1040 Brussels.

DENMARK

Department for Aliens central office: Direktoratet for Udlændinge, Absalonsgade 9, DK-1658 Copenhagen V.

State Employment Service office: Arbejdsformidlingen, Tøndergade 14, DK-1752 Copenhagen V.

Youth information centres (Use-It) central office: Ungdomsinformationen (Use-It), Rådhusstræde 13, DK-1466 Copenhagen K. (This office can provide lists of Arbejdsformidlingen and addresses for accommodation).

ICU (Information Centre for Study and Exchange Programmes), Bremerholm 6, 4., DK-1069 Copenhagen K.

Danish State Hospital: Rigshospitalet, Blegdamsvej 9, DK-2200 Copenhagen N.

Danish Nurses Association: Dansk Sygeplejeråd, PO Box 1084, Vimmelskaftet 38, DK-1161 Copenhagen K.

Danish newspapers: *Jyllands Posten*, Grøndalsvej 3, DK-8260 Viby J.
Berlingske Tidende, Pilestræde, DK-1112 Copenhagen K.

Seasonal work (fruitpicking): Orbaek Mostfabrik (frugtplantage), Odensvej 16, DK-5883 Orbaek.

Workcamps organisation: MS (Mellemfolkeligt Samvirke), Borgergade 14, DK-1300 Copenhagen K.

Coopers and Lybrand I/S, Tax Department, Dyrkøb 3, DK-1166 Copenhagen K. (Provide useful tax information and *Expatriates in Denmark* booklet).

Danish-Irish Society, PO Box 353, DK-1504 Copenhagen V.

Irish Embassy: Østbanegade 21, DK-2100 Copenhagen Ø.

FRANCE

Préfecture de Police, Service des Etrangers, Boulevard de Palais, 75004 Paris.

Youth information centres (CIJ) central office: Centre d'Information et de Documentation de la Jeunesse (CIDJ), 101 quai Branly, 75740 Paris, cedex 15. (This office can provide lists of addresses of ANPE and Préfectures de Police throughout France).

Temporary job agencies (private): Ludéric Services, 20 rue Petrarque, 75016 Paris.

Ludéric Aquitaine, 36 cours du Chapeau Rouge, 33000 Bordeaux.

Sesam, 17 rue Burg, 75018 Paris.

Sesam, 54 rue Pergolese, 75016 Paris.

Hotel and catering publications: L'Hôtellerie, 79 avenue des Champs-Elysées, 75008 Paris.

Syndicat Général des Hôteliers, 22 avenue de la Grande Armée, 75017 Paris. (Accepts jobseeker ads free of charge).

Agricultural employment central agencies (membership fees payable): Centre de Documentation et d'Information Rurale, 92 rue du Dessous des Berges, 75013 Paris.

Jeunesse et Reconstruction, 10 rue de Trévise, 75009 Paris.

Irish Embassy: 12 avenue Foch, 75016 Paris.

Tax information: Conseiller Fiscal, French Embassy, 58 Knightsbridge, London SW1X 7JT.

Lists of hotels and restaurants: French Tourist Office, CIE Tours, 35 Lower Abbey Street, Dublin 1. Tel: 300777.

Alliance Française (French Cultural Centre), 1 Kildare Street, Dublin 2. Tel: 761732.

GERMANY

Federal Employment Service (central placement office, also au pair placement): Zentralstelle für Arbeitsvermittlung, Feuerbachstrasse 42, D-6000 Frankfurt am Main 1.

Youth information centres (Jugendinformationszentrum): Jugendinformationzentrum, Paul Haysestrasse 22, D-8000 Munich 2.

Jugendinformationzentrum, Hokestrasse 9, D-7000 Stuttgart.

Jugend Treff Trantzenwinger (Trantzenwinger Youth Centre), Hintere Insel Schutt 20, D-8500 Nuremberg 1.

Irish Embassy: Godesberger Allee 119, D-5300 Bonn 2.

British Council: Bruderstrasse 7/111, D-8000 Munich 22.

German-Irish Societies:

Deutsch-Irische Gesellschaft e.V., c/o Lorcan MacCumhaill, Postfach 110343, D-4000 Dusseldorf.

Deutsch-Irische Gesellschaft e.V., c/o Ernst Haubach, Ländchenweg 7, D-6200 Wiesbaden-Bierstadt.

Deutsch-Irische Gesellschaft e.V., c/o Karl-Ludwig Wimberger, Postfach 1412, D-5300 Bonn 1.

Irland Verein e.V., Oktaviostrasse 15, D-2000 Hamburg 70.

Deutsch-Irischer Freundeskreis e.V., c/o Werner Friedrichs, Postfach 1366, 7400 Tuebingen.

Deutsch-Irischer Freundeskreis e.V., c/o Hanna Bentfeld, Bruenebrede 47, D-4410 Warendorf 1.

Friedberger Gesellschaft zur Foerderung deutsch-irischer Verständigung e.V., c/o Karl Buxmann, Taunusstrasse 9, D-6361 Reichelsheim 4.

Goethe Institute (German Cultural Institute), 37 Merrion Square, Dublin 2. Tel: 611155. (Administration and library).

62 Fitzwilliam Square, Dublin 2. Tel: 762213. (Language centre).

ITALY

Permesso di Soggiorno: Questura Centrale, Ufficio Stranieri, via Genova 2, Rome.

State Employment Service (Ufficio del Lavoro): Ufficio Collocamento della Manodopera, via Flavia 6, 00147 Rome.

British Council: Palazzo del Drago, via Quattro Fontane 20, 00184 Rome.

Irish Embassy: Largo del Nazareno 3, 00187 Rome.

Tax information: Touche Ross International, 19 Adelaide Road, Dublin 2. Tel: 784833.

Italian State Tourist Office (ENIT), 47 Merrion Square, Dublin 2. Tel: 766397.

Italian Cultural Institute, 11 Fitzwilliam Square, Dublin 2. Tel: 766662.

LUXEMBOURG

State Employment Service: L'Administration de l'Emploi, 34 Avenue de la Porte Neuve, Luxembourg.

Youth information centre: Service Nationale de la Jeunesse, 1 Rue de la Poste (B.P. 707), Luxembourg.

THE NETHERLANDS

State Employment Service (central placement office): Ministerie van Sociale Zaken en Werkgelegenheid, Afdeling Internationale Arbeidsbemiddeling, Postbus 5814, 2280 HV Rijswijk.

Youth centres (BIJK): BIJK, Postbus 15344, 1001 MH Amsterdam. BIJK, Prof. Tulpstraat 2, 1018 HA Amsterdam.

Private temporary employment agencies (Uitzendbureau): Randstad BV, Grote Markt 22, 2511 BJ The Hague.

Randstad BV, Stadhuisplein 39, 3012 AR Rotterdam.

Randstad BV, Wildenborch 5, 1112 XB Diemen.

ASB NZ, Voorburgwal 156, 1012 SJ Amsterdam.

Keser, Herengracht 21, 2511 EG The Hague.

Keser, Mijnsherenlaan 223, 3081 GR Rotterdam.

Keser, Vijzelstraat 7, 1017 HD Amsterdam.

Dutch newspapers: *Dagblad de Telegraaf*, Postbus 376, 1000 EB Amsterdam.

De Volkskrant, Wibautstraat 148-150, 1091 GR Amsterdam.

NRC Handelsblad, Westblaak 180, 3012 KN Rotterdam.

Bulb-picking: Koninklijke Algemene Vereniging voor Bloembollencultuur, 'Bloembollencentrum', Postbus 175, 2180 AG Hillegom.

Farmwork: Landbouwschap, Postbus 85816, 2508 CM The Hague.

Voluntary work organisation: LVV (Landelijke Vereniging van Vrijwilligerscentrales), Potgieterstraat 37, 3532 VP Utrecht.

Education information: NUFFIC (Netherlands University Foundation for International Cooperation), Postbus 90734, 2509 LS The Hague.

Health care: ANOZ (Netherlands General Sickness Fund), Kaap Horndreef 24-28 (Postbus 9069), 3506 GB Utrecht.

Irish Embassy: Dr. Kuyperstraat 9, 2514 BA The Hague.

SPAIN

Youth information and cultural exchange: Instituto de la Juventud (Estafeta Juvenil Internacional), Calle José Ortega y Gasset 71, 28006 Madrid.

British Council: Almagro 5, Madrid 4; Amigo 83, 08021 Barcelona; General San Martin 7, 46004 Valencia.

Irish Embassy: Claudio Coello 73, 28001 Madrid.

Spanish Cultural Institute, 58 Northumberland Road, Dublin 4. Tel: 682024.

ADDRESSES FOR NON-EC EUROPEAN COUNTRIES

AUSTRIA
Regional labour exchanges (landesarbeitsaemter):

Landesarbeitsamt Wien, Weihburggasse 30, A-1010 Vienna.

Landesarbeitsamt Burgenland, Permayerstrasse 10, (Postfach 84), A-7001, Eisenstadt.

Landesarbeitsamt Tirol, Schoepfstrasse 5, Amtsfach, A-6010 Innsbruck.

Landesarbeitsamt Salzburg, Schiesstattgasse 4, (Postfach 185), A-5021 Salzburg.

Landesarbeitsamt Oberoesterreich, Gruberstrasse 63, A-4010 Linz.

Landesarbeitsamt Steiermark, Babenbergerstrasse 33, (Postfach 1068), A-8021 Graz.

Workcamp organisation: Oesterreichische Bauorden, Höernesgasse 4, (Postfach 186), A-1031 Vienna.

Youth information centre: OEKISTA, Tüerkenstrasse 4, A-1090 Vienna.

Irish Embassy: Hilton Centre, A-1030 Vienna.

Summer language teaching camps: Oesterreichische Jugendferienwerk, Alpenstrasse 108a, A-5020 Salzburg.

Local education authorities:

Stadtschulrat fuer Wien, Dr. Karl Renner-Ring 1, A-1014 Vienna.

Landesschulrat fuer Niederoesterreich, Herrengasse 23, A-1010 Vienna.

Landesschulrat fuer Tirol, Neues Landhaus, A-6010 Innsbruck.

Landesschulrat fuer Salzburg, Mozartplatz 10-11, A-5010 Salzburg.

International schools:

American International School, Salmannsdorferstrasse 45-47, A-1190 Vienna.

English Teaching School, Grinzingerstrasse 95, A-1190 Vienna.

Vienna International School, Geymuellergasse 1, A-1190 Vienna.

Austro-Irish Society, c/o Mrs C Arlamovsky, Anastasius Gruen-Gasse, A-1180 Vienna.

Anglo-Austrian Society, 46 Queen Annes Gate, London SW1 H9AU. Tel: 222 0366.

Subscriptions to *Wiener Zeitung* (enclose an international reply coupon): Vertriebsabteilung der Wiener Zeitung, Rennweg 12a, A-1037 Vienna.

British Council: Schenkenstrasse 4, A-1010 Vienna.

FINLAND

Ministry of Labour, International Trainee Exchanges Division, Fabianinkatu 32, PL30, SF-00101 Helsinki.

Finnish Tourist Office, 66 Haymarket, London SW1.

British Council: Eteläesplanadi 22a, SF-00130 Helsinki 13/06.

NORWAY

Norwegian Youth Council (LNU), Farm Guest Programme, Rolf Hofmosgt 18, 0655 Oslo 6.

Norwegian Tourist Office, 20 Pall Mall, London SW1.

British Council: Fridtjof Nansens Plass 5, Oslo 1.

SWEDEN

The Immigration Bureau: Statens Invavdraverk, Box 6113, S-600 06 Norrköping.

Teaching with the Folk University of Sweden: International Language Services, 14 Rollestone Street, Salisbury, Wiltshire SP1 1ED.

Workcamps: Internationella Arbetslag (IAL), Barnangsgaten 23, S-116 41 Stockholm.

Irish Society: Svensk-Irländska Föreningen, Box 7140, S-103 87 Stockholm.

Irish Embassy: Ostermalmsgatan 97, (iv) S-114 59 Stockholm.

British Council: Skarpögatan 6, S-115 127 Stockholm.

SWITZERLAND

Immigration Information: Federal Office for Industry, Crafts and Labour, Manpower and Emigration Division (Emigration and Trainees Section), Bundesgasse 8, 3003 Berne.

Bundesamt für Sozialversicherung, 3003 Berne.

Irish Embassy: Eigerstrasse 71, 3007 Berne.

Swiss Hotel Association Staff Bureau: Société Suisse des Hôteliers, Service de Placement, Case Postale 2657, 3001 Berne.

Jobs in the Alps, PO Box 388, London SW1X 8LX.

Vacation Work International (jobs for students), 9 Park End Street, Oxford OX1 1HJ.

Advertising in Swiss publications: Albert Milhado & Co (Publicitas International Service), 525-527 Fulham Road, London SW6. Tel: 358 7723.

Swiss newspapers (German-speaking): *Berner Zeitung, Bund* (Berne); *Neue Zurcher Zeitung, Tages-Anzeiger* (Zürich); *Basler Zeitung* (Basle); *Luzerner Neueste Nachrichten* (Lucerne).

Swiss newspapers (French-speaking): *Journal de Genève, Tribune de Gènève, La Suisse* (Geneva); *Tribune-Le Matin, Gazette de Lausanne, 24 Heures* (Lausanne).

Swiss newspapers (Italian-speaking): *Corriere del Ticino* (Lugano); *Popolo e Liberta* (Bellinzona).

TURKEY

Workcamps and youth travel: Çenctur, Yerebatan Caddesi 15/3, Sultanahmet, Istanbul.

International Volunteers Exchange Service, c/o 7 Tur, Abdulhakhamit Caddesi 2/3, Taksim, Istanbul.

IAESTE Turkey, ITU Maden Fukultesi, Tesvikiye, Istanbul.

English teaching: Turkish-American Association, Cinnah Caddesi 20, Kavaklidere, Ankara.

British Council: Kat 2, Ege Han, Cumhüriyet Caddesi 22/24, Elmadağ, Istanbul.

English language newspaper: *The Daily News*, Tunas Caddesi 49/7, Kavaklidere, Ankara.

Turkish Embassy, Culture and Information Counsellor's Office, 170-173 Piccadilly, London W1V 9DD.

8
Useful Publications

Many of the embassies of the countries included in this book provide information for the aspiring worker, tourist or student. Embassy handouts are usually in the form of an information sheet or form letter, and are often free. They provide a useful source of references and further addresses. The following is a selection of what is available.

Austrian Embassy, Dublin: Two form letters, one on finding work in general and one for teachers (2pp each, useful addresses, though a rather discouraging tone).

Belgian Embassy, Dublin: *Camping 89* (a list of campsites, facilities and prices), *Hotels 89* (a similar list for the more upmarket traveller), *Belgium — Historic Cities* (a very useful tourist information booklet). They have no specific information on finding work.

Danish Embassy, Dublin: *Working in Denmark* (2pp, fairly comprehensive), *Ireland-Denmark: A Business Guide.*

French Embassy, Dublin: *Working in France* (8pp, useful addresses).

German Embassy, Dublin: *Residence and Work in the Federal Republic of Germany* (2pp, refers one to Irish organisations), *Information Booklet for Migrant Workers and Emigrants, Bundesverwaltungsamt* (99pp, excellent background information, though nothing on actually finding a job).

Italian Embassy, Dublin: *General Information on Living and Working in Italy* (3pp, rather limited information).

Netherlands Embassy, Dublin: *General Information* (4pp), *Holland — Surprisingly Versatile* (a glossy, bland tourist booklet).

Spanish Embassy, Dublin: *Working in Spain* (1 page form letter on visas), *Taking up Residence in Spain* (9pp booklet, mostly about customs regulations).

Swedish Embassy, Dublin: *Work Permits in Sweden* (8pp, the visa regulations in detail). Fact sheets and booklets full of statistical information about all aspects of life in Sweden are also available.

Swiss Embassy, Dublin: *Information for persons wishing to take up employment in Switzerland* (2pp, detailed information and addresses).

Europeans, you have rights. Commission of the European Communities, Luxembourg, 1987.

Student Handbook, Higher Education in the European Community. Commission of the European Communities, Luxembourg, 1988.

Social Security for Migrant Workers. EC Information Office, Dublin.

SW49: Social Security in the EC. Dept of Social Welfare, Dublin.

Work Your Way Around the World, by Susan Griffith. Vacation-Work, Oxford 1987. IR£8.25, 383pp. This is one of a number of books published by Vacation-Work. All of them are packed with addresses and advice for young people who want to try to find jobs elsewhere. Other useful titles include *The Directory of Work and Study in Developing Countries, Working in Ski Resorts — Europe, Vacation Traineeships for Students, The Directory of Summer Jobs Abroad* and *The Directory of Jobs and Careers Abroad.*

Working Abroad, The Daily Telegraph Guide to Working and Living Overseas, by Godfrey Golzen. Kogan Page, London 1988. IR£9.45, 347pp. This book, really intended for the businessman, deals with international price comparisons and living conditions — including the availibility of servants — all over the world. Quite useful, but expensive and full of advertising. The yearly updating is patchy.

Young Visitors series. Published by official youth information organisations in EC countries, in association with ERICYA. This series is a recent development, bound to be updated and improved. Editions for other EC countries, including Ireland, are due in 1989. Though they vary in quality, they are an excellent source of background information and addresses for anyone going to one of the countries involved. The full titles are: *Belgium, Use It 87, Guide for Young Visitors to Denmark,*

Hello France, Young Visitors to the Netherlands, Spain for Young Visitors, Young Visitors to Britain.

TIDE Directory, by the Youth Emigration Action Group, Dublin 1987. IR£10. Available from Emigration Advice, 1a Cathedral Street, Dublin 1. A worthy attempt to explain the position facing the emigrant in 10 countries, with information on getting work, accommodation and social welfare.

Over in Europe, by Chris O'Malley, MEP. The Orchard Press, Dublin, 1988. IR£4.95, 127pp. The subtitle sums it up: '*The issues facing Ireland in the European Community*'. Recommended reading for anyone concerned about the future of this country and 1992.

Across the Frontiers: Ireland in the 1990s, Ed. Richard Kearney. Wolfhound Press, Dublin, 1988. IR£8.95, 280pp. A series of essays which explores the political and philosophical implications of greater European involvement in Irish affairs.

AUSTRALIA: A HANDBOOK FOR LIVING AND WORKING DOWN UNDER
by *Fiachra O Marcaigh* and *Jessica Classon*

The definitive guide to Australia for the traveller, tourist or emigrant. And its all in here — how to get there and what to do when you arrive . . . without question a MUST for any person who has given even a passing thought to visiting or emigrating to the 'Lucky Country' — so says broadcaster Mike Murphy in his introduction to this handy handbook, packed with excellent information and advice. The chapters cover:

- What's all this about Australia?
- Getting in — Visas
- Too far to swim — Getting there
- Your swag — What to bring
- A place to stay
- Yakka — Work and how to find it
- The system
- Settling in
- Dunnies, dingoes and dinky dis — The language
- What's where — Cities and states
- Going walkabout — Holidays and travel
- History of Australia — The first 45 million years
- Useful addresses
- Books about Australia

As Mike Murphy says, if his research team for the TV programme *Murphy's Australia* had had this book, their work load would have been cut in half.